U.S. History
People and Events
1607–1865

By

GEORGE LEE

COPYRIGHT © 2005 Mark Twain Media, Inc.

ISBN   10-digit: 1-58037-336-4
          13-digit: 978-1-58037-336-4

Printing No. CD-404039

Mark Twain Media, Inc., Publishers
Distributed by Carson-Dellosa Publishing LLC

Revised/Previously published as *Decisions That Shaped America: 1607–1865*

Visit us at www.carsondellosa.com

Table of Contents

1 Time Line
4 Introduction
5 Queen Isabella Appoints an Admiral
7 Captain John Smith Saves Jamestown
9 Pilgrims Write the *Mayflower Compact*
11 Religious Toleration Becomes the Law in Maryland
13 The Zenger Trial and Freedom of the Press
15 Colonists Develop a Diverse Work Force
17 Washington Joins Braddock's Expedition
19 James Otis Fights the Stamp Act
21 Sam Adams' Tea Party
23 Patrick Henry Demands Liberty or Death
25 The Declaration of Independence Is Signed
27 Washington Stages a Surprise Attack on Trenton
29 Saratoga: Little People Mess Up Grand Plans
31 Benedict Arnold Betrays the Cause
33 A Peace Treaty Is Made With England in 1783
35 The States Form a Confederation
37 Old Soldiers Threaten Civilian Rule
39 The Calling of the Constitutional Convention
41 Washington Stays Calm in Stormy Times
43 Eli Whitney Invents the Cotton Gin
45 Matthew Lyon Defies the Sedition Act
47 Opportunity Knocks: Jefferson Responds
49 John Marshall Declares an Act of Congress Unconstitutional
51 "Fulton's Folly" Changes Transportation
53 The United States Declares War on England in 1812
55 The Missouri Compromise Is Passed
57 The Election Where Second Place Was Good Enough to Win

59 Americans Invest in Internal Improvements
61 A "Man of the People" Is Elected President
63 The Five Civilized Tribes Are Moved West
65 Jackson Declares War on Nullifiers and the Second Bank of the United States
67 Some Slaves Refuse to Give in to Their Masters
69 The North Develops an Industrial Economy
71 Houston Leads Texans to Independence
73 Americans Take an Interest in Oregon
75 Abolitionists Act, Congress Reacts
77 Nicholas Trist Makes Peace With Mexico
79 Sutter's Secret Is Told—A Gold Rush Follows
81 Daniel Webster Delivers the Seventh of March Speech
83 *Uncle Tom's Cabin* Is Published
85 The Nation Focuses on "Bleeding Kansas"
87 Buchanan Is Elected in 1856
89 John Brown Attacks Harpers Ferry
91 South Carolina Secedes
93 Lincoln Asks for 75,000 Volunteers
95 African-Americans Become Part of the War
97 The South Scores Some Wins
99 July 4, 1863—A Day of Northern Victories
101 Women Join the War Effort on Both Sides
103 Booth Kills Lincoln
105 The Bragging Contest
108 You Decide
112 Answer Keys
126 Suggestions for Further Reading

ii

Time Line

We tell the story of our lives by dates. I was born in _____, started school in _____, and in _____, we moved to our new home. Dates also help us understand history. By dates, we can look at the past and see the order in which events occurred. They also help us keep historical events in sequence. This time line covers events from 1492 to 1865.

1492	Christopher Columbus sails to the New World.
1519–21	Hernando Cortés conquers Mexico.
1533	Francisco Pizarro conquers the Incas in Peru.
1585	Roanoke Island colony is established; it disappears by 1591.
1588	Battle of Spanish Armada proves English naval power.
1603	James I succeeds Elizabeth I as the English ruler.
1607	Jamestown colony is established in Virginia.
1619	First Africans arrive in Jamestown and are sold as servants.
1620	Plymouth Colony is established by Pilgrims.
1624	The Dutch establish New Netherland colony at the Hudson River.
1630	Massachusetts Bay Colony is established by the Puritans.
1637	Pequot War in New England
1649–60	Puritan rule in England
1660	Charles II restores the monarchy in England.
1664	New Netherland captured by the English and renamed New York.
1676	Bacon's Rebellion in Virginia
1682	La Salle sails down the Mississippi River and claims Louisiana for France.
1688	Glorious Revolution in England; William and Mary are now rulers.
1689–97	King William's War
1692	Witchcraft trials in Salem, Massachusetts
1702-13	Queen Anne's War
1744–48	King George's War
1754	French and Indian War begins.
1756–63	Seven Years' War in Europe
1759	Quebec is captured by the English.
1763–66	Pontiac's Rebellion
1763	Proclamation Line is drawn.
1764	Parliament passes the Sugar Act to raise money.
1765	Stamp Act; Stamp Act Congress
1766	Stamp Act is repealed.
1767	Townshend Duties
1770	Boston Massacre
1773	Tea Act is passed by Parliament; Boston Tea Party
1774	Intolerable Acts passed by Parliament; General Gage arrives.
1775	Battles of Lexington and Concord; Continental Congress; Battle of Bunker Hill
1776	Second Continental Congress; Declaration of Independence; Battle of Trenton
1777	Battle of Princeton; Battle of Saratoga; French Alliance

Time Line (cont.)

1781	Articles of Confederation are approved; Battle of Yorktown
1783	Treaty of Paris gives United States independence.
1785	Land Ordinance divides Northwest Territory into townships.
1786	Shays' Rebellion
1787	Northwest Ordinance; Constitutional Convention
1789	Constitution is ratified; Washington is inaugurated; French Revolution begins.
1791	Bill of Rights is ratified.
1793	Cotton gin is invented.
1794	Whiskey Rebellion in Pennsylvania is put down.
1795	Battle of Fallen Timbers; Jay's Treaty
1796	Adams is elected president.
1797	XYZ Affair angers Americans.
1798	Alien and Sedition Acts
1800	Gabriel's slave revolt in Virginia; Jefferson is elected.
1803	Louisiana Purchase; *Marbury v. Madison* decision
1804–06	Lewis and Clark Expedition
1807	*Chesapeake* Affair; Embargo Act is passed.
1811	Battle of Tippecanoe; War Hawks control Congress.
1812	War of 1812
1813	Battle of Lake Erie; Battle of Thames
1814	Hartford Convention; Treaty of Ghent ends the War of 1812.
1815	Battle of New Orleans
1816	Second Bank of the United States is chartered.
1817	Rush-Bagot Agreement reduces armed forces on Great Lakes.
1818	United States and England agree on boundary at 49° from Lake of the Woods to the crest of Rocky Mountains.
1820	Missouri Compromise
1821	Adams-Onis Treaty transfers Florida from Spain to the United States.
1822	Santa Fe trade opens.
1823	Monroe Doctrine
1825	Erie Canal is completed.
1828	Jackson is elected president.
1830	Webster-Hayne debate; Indian Removal Bill passes.
1831	Nat Turner's Rebellion
1832	Jackson vetoes recharter of Second Bank of the United States.
1836	Texas War for Independence
1837	Panic of 1837
1841	First wagon trains travel to Oregon and California.
1844	James K. Polk is elected president.
1845	Texas is annexed.
1846	Oregon boundary is set at 49°; Mexican War; Wilmot Proviso
1848	Mexican War ends: United States acquires California and New Mexico.

Time Line (cont.)

1849	Gold rush to California
1850	Compromise of 1850
1852	*Uncle Tom's Cabin* is published.
1854	Kansas-Nebraska Act is passed; Republican party is formed.
1857	*Dred Scott* decision; Panic of 1857
1859	Harpers Ferry is raided by John Brown.
1860	Abraham Lincoln is elected president; South Carolina secedes.
1861	Ft. Sumter is fired upon; Lincoln calls for 75,000 volunteers; Battle of Bull Run
1862	Battles at Shiloh, Second Bull Run, and Antietam; Pacific Railroad Act; Homestead Act
1863	Emancipation Proclamation; Battles of Vicksburg and Gettysburg; New York draft riots; Gettysburg Address
1864	Sherman's march through Georgia; Lincoln is reelected.
1865	Robert E. Lee surrenders; Lincoln is killed, and Vice President Andrew Johnson replaces him; Congress adopts the Thirteenth Amendment.

U.S. Population (in millions)

Year	Population
1790	3.92
1800	5.30
1810	7.23
1820	9.63
1830	12.86
1840	17.06
1850	23.19
1860	31.44

U.S. Railroad Mileage

Year	Mileage
1830	23
1835	1,098
1840	2,818
1845	4,633
1850	9,021
1855	18,374
1860	30,626

Introduction

Decisions—we make them all the time. However, we don't usually think of them as being important; in fact, many are not. But the consequences of our decisions can be far-reaching because they may stretch beyond ourselves to affect others. If a young person prefers to buy a CD by the ABCs rather than one made by the XYZs, that puts money in the ABCs' pocket. If everyone buys only the ABCs' CDs, the XYZs are out of business.

Decisions made by one person often affect others as well. A young person's decision to take drugs may be devastating to himself and his family. Another family's future may be decided by someone the family doesn't even know and has never heard of, but this mystery person decides to open a factory or close one or to buy more (or less) of the products this person produces.

Some decisions have affected not only individuals and those with whom they come in contact but have changed history. Most of the time, the person making the decision was thinking about himself or herself and what was to his or her advantage at that moment. He or she was not thinking in terms of how people hundreds of years from then would react to it. Some decisions turn out for the better, some for the worse. At times, there were surprising side effects. Eli Whitney's cotton gin is a good example. He was not thinking about how it would create a new demand for slaves. He was only interested in helping farmers clean seeds from their cotton.

As we look at decisions made by people of the past, we need to realize that they were products of their time and place, just as we are. We may not approve of things they did, but we cannot judge them by the standards of our time. We can't imagine any intelligent person thinking slaveholding is fine, so we assume they must have felt guilty for owning human property. However, if they grew up in the South before the Civil War, slavery was part of their society, and they may never have met a person who opposed slavery. No one asked what slaves wanted, but eventually some African-American men and women made decisions affecting themselves and history. Fighting duels was another sign of the times, but it wasn't much different than the death-defying risks some people take today. The role of women was much more restricted than in the modern world. Men thought that women were there to cook, tend the garden, and produce children. They thought it was a waste of time to educate women or listen to them. As a result, a woman's role was very limited in making major decisions that affected the nation. Nevertheless, some women made or began making major breakthroughs.

This book is about decisions made before 1865. The nation was young, and in some ways it was different from what it became—different even from any nation in existence at the time. Crèvecoeur asked, "What is this new man, this American?" Perhaps one way to answer that question is to look at decisions that made America what it was and what it would become.

The information in this book is correlated with the National Council of Social Studies (NCSS™) curriculum standards and the National Standards of History (NSH). It also supports the No Child Left Behind (NCLB) initiative. Relevant websites are given in each chapter for students to use in researching the topics further.

Queen Isabella Appoints an Admiral

Christopher Columbus

Queen Isabella of Spain studied the face of the sailor who stood before her. He seemed self-assured, experienced, and certainly bold, but was he insane for what he wanted to do, and would she be wise to back him?

In 1492, Isabella was 41 years old and had already proven herself as a woman who knew what she wanted. Born into the royal family of Castile, her family had tried to marry her off twice while she was very young. One prospective husband died when she was 10, the other died on his way to their wedding when she was 15. In 1469, she married the man she chose, Ferdinand of Aragon, and together they began to conquer the rest of Spain. She knew the look in the sailor's eye—that desire to achieve and conquer shone in her eyes as well. Her advisors told her the sailor was doomed to failure. Ships were not strong enough, and Asia was too far away.

Christopher Columbus, a sailor, was also 41 years old. He came from a humble Italian family of weavers. He had been drawn to the sea at an early age. When he was 15, the ship on which he sailed was attacked by pirates, and he landed in Portugal. There he learned valuable skills: reading, writing, navigation, and seamanship. In 1479, he married and for a time worked as a merchant. But the sea called to him, so he boarded a ship sailing to Africa's Gold Coast. This ocean voyage would give him valuable experience.

To Columbus, it seemed logical to assume that one could reach China by sailing west, and the treasures of the Orient would enrich the person and nation that was first to arrive. Most educated people knew the world was round; that wasn't the problem. The question was whether the ships of the time, caravels, could make such a long journey. Columbus tried to persuade the rulers of Portugal, Spain, and then England to sponsor the trip, but all rejected him. Again, he returned to Spain where the war to remove the Moslems from Grenada was ending. Again, the queen turned him down, so he started to leave for Portugal. But a messenger caught up with him and told him to return to the palace. The queen had decided in his favor; he would be given the title "Admiral of the Ocean Seas" and would receive ten percent of the revenues from anything he found. In a dramatic gesture, she said she would sell her jewels if necessary to fund the trip, but money was raised elsewhere. With three small ships, Columbus set sail in August, 1492.

RESULTS: Columbus discovered a small island on October 12 and assumed he was somewhere near India; for that reason, he called the friendly Taino natives on the island "Indians." He would make four voyages all together but proved to be a better explorer than ruler. There were many complaints about his using Indians as slaves and the harsh way in which he and his family ruled. In 1499, he was taken to Spain in chains. Later his title and money were restored. Queen Isabella died in 1504; Columbus died in 1506. To his dying day, Columbus was sure his discoveries were on the outskirts of China.

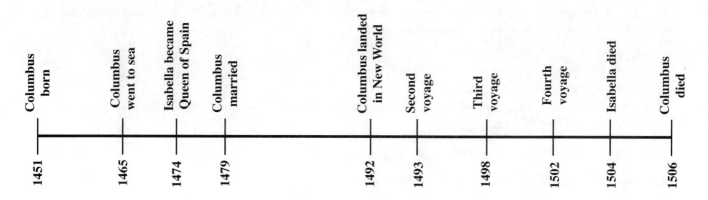

Columbus born	Columbus went to sea	Isabella became Queen of Spain	Columbus married	Columbus landed in New World	Second voyage	Third voyage	Fourth voyage	Isabella died	Columbus died
1451	1465	1474	1479	1492	1493	1498	1502	1504	1506

Name: _____ Date: _____

Queen Isabella Appoints an Admiral: Reinforcement

Directions: Complete the following activities, essays, and challenges on your own paper.

ACTIVITIES:

1. Have students create a map of the four voyages of Columbus and those of other explorers. Notice that at no time did Columbus come to any part of what is now the United States.
2. Have students look at models or pictures of caravels found in encyclopedias or on the Internet and draw pictures of these ships.

ESSAYS:

1. You are Columbus writing a letter to the queen. Describe the trip you are planning and your qualifications to command the expedition.
2. You are Isabella, and people are asking you why you have agreed to let Columbus make this trip. What reasons would you give?
3. A friend of yours has signed on to go on a voyage with Columbus, and he wants you to go. If you want to go, write a letter to your mother explaining why you would like to go. If you don't want to go, write a letter to your friend and explain why you are turning him down.

CHALLENGES:

1. In what year was Columbus born?
2. In what year was Isabella almost married the first time?
3. What had been Columbus' longest trip before he sailed in 1492?
4. Who was Spain fighting in 1492?
5. How many times was Columbus turned down before he got approval?
6. Before his title of "Admiral of the Ocean Seas" meant anything, what would Columbus have to do?
7. What were two good reasons that Isabella could have given for not helping Columbus when he asked the first time?
8. Why did Columbus call the natives he met "Indians"?
9. Why didn't Columbus take any pride in discovering a "new world"?
10. If you were Columbus, what questions would you have to consider in planning your trip?
11. When we look at the globe, it is obvious that Columbus is nowhere near China or India. What could have caused him to be so far off in his calculations?

NATIONAL STANDARDS CORRELATIONS:

NCSS VIi: (Power, Authority, & Governance) Give examples and explain how governments attempt to achieve their stated ideals at home and abroad.

NSH Era 1, Standard 2: How early European exploration and colonization resulted in cultural and ecological interactions among previously unconnected peoples

WEBSITES:

http://www.ibiblio.org/expo/1492.exhibit/overview.html
"Outline of Objects and Topics in 1492: An Ongoing Voyage Exhibit," The Library of Congress

http://memory.loc.gov/ammem/gmdhtml/dsxphome.html
"Discovery and Exploration," The Library of Congress

http://memory.loc.gov/ammem/gmdhtml/gmdhome.html
"Map Collections: 1500–2004," The Library of Congress

Captain John Smith Saves Jamestown

John Smith

Other nations besides Spain were interested in establishing colonies, especially after Cortés conquered the Aztecs of Mexico and Pizarro the Incas of Peru. In both cases, they took large quantities of gold from the natives. Portuguese sailors moved down the coast of Africa, and their ships came back with gold, ivory, and slaves. England was also interested, but their explorer, John Cabot, found no great wealth, and only a few Englishmen were interested in colonizing. Sir Humphrey Gilbert tried to establish a colony in Newfoundland in 1583, but he died at sea, and the settlers returned after a cold winter. In 1587, Sir Walter Raleigh sent 117 settlers to Roanoke Island (North Carolina), but this colony disappeared.

Establishing colonies was too expensive for any one person to afford. A new system developed: the joint stock company. Groups of people would each put up part of the cost and receive a share of the profits. The Muscovy Company traded in Russia and the East India Company in India. In 1606, the London Company was formed, and it sent 144 settlers to develop a coastal settlement at Jamestown in Virginia. One of those men was 27-year-old John Smith.

Smith's motto was *Vincere est vivere* (To conquer is to live). He had been tossed overboard from a sinking ship and had fought the Turks. The Turks captured him and held him as a slave with a chain around his neck. He escaped and finally returned to England in 1604. When he learned about the expedition to create a new colony, he signed on. He was supposed to be a member of the council for the colony, but after arguing with the ship's captain, Smith finished the voyage in chains.

Smith was released after a jury trial. In December 1607, Smith was captured by the Native Americans living in the area, but the chief's daughter, Pocahontas, risked her life to save his. When he returned to Jamestown, he was arrested and charged with causing the deaths of the two men who had gone with him into Native-American country. After he was found not guilty, he was elected council president.

The colony was in danger of starvation, despite the fact that the soil was good and plenty of food could be found. Six-foot-long sturgeon swam past. Deer were abundant, and turkeys weighing 70 pounds were nearby. But the men who came were looking for quick riches, so they wandered up and down the beaches looking for gold nuggets. They wanted to get rich and go home. They ignored the danger they were in. Smith ordered that every man must work or would receive no food. The colonists began to grow blisters on their hands as they tilled fields and built houses. After Smith was injured by an explosion, he returned to England in 1609. He returned to North America in 1612 and drew maps of a region he named "New England." He was captured by pirates and then by the French in 1615. When he got home, he spent the rest of his life quietly writing books about his adventures.

RESULTS: Later, leaders of Virginia would continue to force settlers to work. The London Company never made any money from their efforts, but John Rolfe would take a local plant, tobacco, and export it to England. Pocahontas later married John Rolfe.

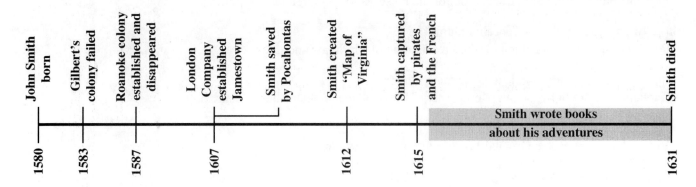

John Smith born	Gilbert's colony failed	Roanoke colony established and disappeared	London Company established Jamestown	Smith saved by Pocahontas	Smith created "Map of Virginia"	Smith captured by pirates and the French		Smith died
							Smith wrote books about his adventures	
1580	1583	1587	1607		1612	1615		1631

Name: _____ Date: _____

Captain John Smith Saves Jamestown: Reinforcement

Directions: Complete the following activities, essays, and challenges on your own paper.

ACTIVITIES:

1. On a map, identify the places John Smith went. Ask what drives a man to take the risks he did.
2. Research the Lost Colony, Powhatan, and Pocahontas.

ESSAYS:

1. You overhear a stockholder in the London Company talking with a man who has signed up to establish the colony at Jamestown. What would he say was the duty of the settler?
2. You are one of the settlers who has been in Jamestown from the beginning. Write a letter to a friend in England. Describe your experience.
3. To be a great leader, does a person have to be popular? How might Smith and others have handled the situation so there would not have been so many complaints among the settlers?

CHALLENGES:

1. Why did joint stock companies rather than private individuals start colonies?
2. How many times was John Smith held as someone's prisoner?
3. Why was Cabot's voyage to the New World discouraging to those thinking about colonizing America?
4. Who established the famous "Lost Colony"?
5. What reason did the English have for thinking there would be gold in the New World?
6. Why did the settlers in Jamestown almost starve?
7. What was the name of the Native American girl who saved Smith's life? Whom did she marry?
8. What kind of people came to Jamestown? How long did they plan to stay?
9. What are sturgeon?
10. Captain Smith was not very popular, even though he was saving the lives of the settlers. How would you account for that?

NATIONAL STANDARDS CORRELATIONS:

NCSS Id: (Culture) Explain why individuals and groups respond differently to their physical and social environments and/or changes to them on the basis of shared assumptions, values, and beliefs.

NSH Era 2, Standard 1: Why the Americas attracted Europeans, why they brought enslaved Africans to their colonies, and how Europeans struggled for control of North America and the Caribbean

WEBSITES:

http://www.apva.org/history/jsmith.html
"Captain John Smith," The Association for the Preservation of Virginia Antiquities

http://www.apva.org/history/pocahont.html
"Pocahontas," The Association for the Preservation of Virginia Antiquities

http://www.history.org/foundation/journal/smith.cfm
"Captain John Smith by Dennis Montgomery," The Colonial Williamsburg Foundation

http://www.virtualjamestown.org/maps1.html
"Virtual Jamestown: The Original Maps," virtualjamestown.org

Pilgrims Write the *Mayflower Compact*

When Henry VIII created the Church of England (Anglican), many of his people were unhappy. Catholics did not like the king assuming the power of the pope, but the greatest problem came from citizens who felt the new church was too similar to the Catholic Church. They were called "Puritans" because they wanted to "purify" the church and remove statues, bishops, and rituals. Others went even further—they wanted to separate from the Anglican church and were known as "Separatists." Both groups followed the teachings of John Calvin, who stressed strict obedience to the Ten Commandments. They also believed that God would punish nations that did not follow Him. Therefore, they would not obey those leaders, even if they were kings. They would rather die than surrender to immoral laws.

The Mayflower

Both Puritans and Separatists found life under the Stuart rulers especially hard. The Stuarts were too much like the Catholics as far as they were concerned. Because of their opposition, they faced beatings, brandings, loss of property, and even death. They longed for the day when they would be able to practice religion in their own way.

In 1608, a group of Separatists called Pilgrims went to Holland, which was more tolerant of their views. However, the only jobs they could get were as day laborers, and their children grew up more Dutch than English. Rather than return to England to live, they made a deal with the London Company. The merchants would pay for their trip to North America; after seven years, they and the company would divide the profits.

The captain of their ship, the *Mayflower,* took them to the coast of Massachusetts. The ship lay anchor at the spot they named "Plymouth," the name of the port from which they had sailed. However, they had landed north of the London Company's territory, so they had no legal authority to the land they claimed. Many of the settlers were not Pilgrims, including their military commander, Miles Standish, so their religion could not be the bond holding them together. They feared attack by Native Americans, the French, or the Spanish. Their situation required that everyone conform to certain rules of conduct. They knew that either they worked together, or all would die.

An agreement known as the *Mayflower Compact* was drawn up and was signed by 41 men on November 11, 1620. They agreed to form a civil body and to abide by the "just and equal laws" that would be passed.

RESULTS: Plymouth's settlers were not well prepared to survive in a wilderness. Despite able leadership from William Bradford, the colony remained poor and small until it was absorbed by the Massachusetts Bay Colony in 1691. Plymouth's greatest contribution to history may have been the *Mayflower Compact.* By agreeing to accept the rule of the majority and by putting it into written form, Plymouth's settlers set a precedent for written constitutions that would follow.

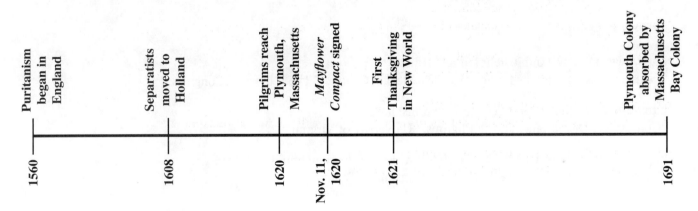

Puritanism began in England	Separatists moved to Holland	Pilgrims reach Plymouth, Massachusetts	*Mayflower Compact* signed	First Thanksgiving in New World	Plymouth Colony absorbed by Massachusetts Bay Colony
1560	1608	1620	Nov. 11, 1620	1621	1691

Name: _____ Date: _____

Pilgrims Write the *Mayflower Compact*: Reinforcement

Directions: Complete the following activities, essays, and challenges on your own paper.

ACTIVITIES:

1. Most Americans associate Thanksgiving with the Pilgrims. Have students research the origins of Thanksgiving. What was served at the first Thanksgiving meal?
2. Have students look up information on Calvinism, William Bradford, and the Plymouth Colony.

ESSAYS:

1. The dictionary describes a "pilgrim" as a wanderer who travels to a holy place. How do you think this definition fits the Pilgrims who came to America?
2. In a situation like the one they faced, do you feel people should have to give up some of their freedom of choice?
3. You are one of the Pilgrims sitting on a ship at Plymouth. Write a letter to a friend in England. Describe your excitement, your fears, and the ocean voyage you have taken.

CHALLENGES:

1. What is an easy way to remember who the Puritans were?
2. What is an easy way to remember who the Separatists were?
3. What church did Henry VIII create?
4. How did the Puritans get along with kings?
5. Why did the Pilgrims go to Holland?
6. Why did they come to America rather than return to live in England?
7. Who was their military leader? From whom was he supposed to protect them?
8. Why did they choose the name "Plymouth" for their colony?
9. There were 101 passengers on the *Mayflower*. How could only 41 of them make an agreement for all?
10. Who was the best leader of the Plymouth Colony?

NATIONAL STANDARDS CORRELATIONS:

NCSS VIb: (Power, Authority, & Governance) Describe the purpose of government and how its powers are acquired, used, and justified.
NSH Era 1, Standard 1: Comparative characteristics of societies in the Americas, Western Europe, and Western Africa that increasingly interacted after 1450

WEBSITES:

http://www.loc.gov/exhibits/religion/rel101.html
"I. America as a Religious Refuge: The Seventeenth Century," The Library of Congress

http://xroads.virginia.edu/~CAP/puritan/purhist.html
"Context and Developments: The Pilgrims," University of Virginia

http://www.nhc/rtp.nc.us:8080/tserve/eighteen/ekeyinfo/puritan.htm
"Puritanism and Predestination," National Humanities Center

Religious Toleration Becomes the Law in Maryland

Lord Baltimore

In 1632, George Calvert (Lord Baltimore) was given a grant of land north of Virginia. He named it Maryland. He had two ideas in mind: to gain wealth from it and to provide a place where Catholics could practice their faith. His plans were in serious trouble by 1649. Problems with Charles I had forced many Puritans to leave England. Some came to Maryland, where they and other Protestants outnumbered Catholics. In 1642, civil war broke out in England between the king and Parliament, which was controlled by Puritans. It ended seven years later, with Parliament winning and the king executed. Lord Baltimore had good reason to fear that his plan to protect Maryland's Catholics was in danger.

Religious toleration as we would think of it was not acceptable at that time in Europe, England, or America. To oppose the approved, established church was a sign that a person was unpatriotic. Sometimes wars would be fought over religion. Many countries restricted those who openly disagreed with the national church. In colonial Massachusetts, a man could not vote or hold public office if he did not belong to the church. Part of everyone's taxes went to pay the cost of the church, regardless of whether he was a member or not. Those who did not accept the doctrines of the established church (dissenters) wanted the system changed.

In Massachusetts, Roger Williams had argued that church and state should be separate and government had no right to punish those who did not attend church. Everyone liked Williams, even the governor, but he was forced to leave the colony. With a group of his friends, he formed the new colony Rhode Island in 1636. People of many different religious beliefs settled in Rhode Island—including Jews, Quakers, and non-believers—and lived in harmony. Lord Baltimore was not willing to go that far in allowing freedom, but he knew that unless he acted soon, Parliament or the Protestant majority in Maryland would take the situation out of his hands.

His Act of Toleration provided that any Christian could worship as he pleased. Anyone who insulted another person's religion would be fined. If he could not pay the fine, he would be publicly whipped and jailed.

RESULTS: The Act of Toleration did not last long. Soon Puritans took control of the legislature and passed laws restricting the Catholics. But the Act of Toleration was a beginning for people to accept religions that did not agree with their own views.

There have been times in American history when different religions were very unpopular, and those who were members suffered hardships for their beliefs. But even unpopular groups are protected by the Constitution's First Amendment, which allows the freedom of religion.

Today, America has not only the Protestants and Catholics that would have been protected by the Act of Toleration, but many other groups it left out: Jews, Moslems, Hindus, and others. America is a land where religious diversity can be a blessing, not a curse.

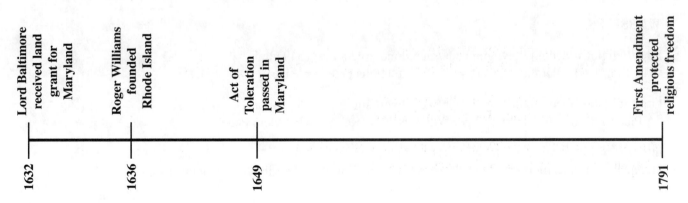

Lord Baltimore received land grant for Maryland — 1632

Roger Williams founded Rhode Island — 1636

Act of Toleration passed in Maryland — 1649

First Amendment protected religious freedom — 1791

Name: _____ Date: _____

Religious Toleration Becomes the Law in Maryland: Reinforcement

Directions: Complete the following activities, essays, and challenges on your own paper.

ACTIVITIES:

1. Search newspaper or magazine articles for stories about places where religious violence commonly takes place.
2. Have students look at the First Amendment and its two restrictions on government actions in restricting or promoting religion. Ask what could happen if such limits had not been placed.

ESSAYS:

1. Is it important for people to have the right to choose their own religion? Why?
2. The Act of Toleration punished people who insulted someone else's religion. Do you think that would be a good policy today? Why or why not?
3. Pretend that the United States is at war with a nation that worships the moon and thinks it is made of green cheese. How would you feel about the moon worshippers who attend school with you?

CHALLENGES:

1. What city in Maryland does the Act of Toleration remind you of and why?
2. Who won the English Civil War?
3. What happened to the king (Charles I)?
4. What group was Lord Baltimore trying to help? Why?
5. Who was forced to leave Massachusetts because of his beliefs?
6. Where did the man in question 5 go?
7. What happened to people who insulted someone else's religion?
8. What restrictions in Massachusetts limited those who did not belong to the established church?
9. What are some of the churches in your town? How do they get along?
10. Why was there no concern about Moslems and Hindus having the right to worship when the Act of Toleration was in effect?

NATIONAL STANDARDS CORRELATIONS:

NCSS Xb: (Civic Ideals & Practices) Identify and interpret sources and examples of the rights and responsibilities of citizens.
NSH Era 2, Standard 2: How political, religious, and social institutions emerged in the English colonies

WEBSITES:

http://religiousfreedom.lib.virginia.edu/sacred/md_toleration_1649.html
"The Maryland Toleration Act (1649)," The Religious Freedom Page

http://religiousfreedom.lib.virginia.edu/sacred/williams_plea_1644.html
"A Plea for Religious Liberty: Roger Williams," The Religious Freedom Page

http://www.loc.gov/exhibits/religion/rel101-2.html
"I. America as a Religious Refuge: The Seventeenth Century," The Library of Congress

The Zenger Trial and Freedom of the Press

Andrew Hamilton

John Peter Zenger had reason to be afraid as his case was called. Opposing him was the great power of Governor William Cosby, the prosecutor, and the judges. Even with public opinion on his side, it seemed he was sure to lose until a famous lawyer came to his rescue, and the trivial case of the *Crown v. Zenger* became a page in the history of freedom of the press.

Peter Zenger was 13 when his family came to America from Germany in 1710. His mother apprenticed him to a printer so he might learn a trade. In 1725, he became a partner in the *New-York Weekly Journal*.

There were very few newspapers in the colonies, and those that existed seldom criticized the government. People did not know whether or not there was corruption because newspapers did not want to offend the persons who paid for the printing of public notices. Although colonial governors were chosen by the king or the colonial proprietor, some colonies did have good governors. However, New York had Governor William Cosby, a corrupt man who used his power to get rich. Most people feared him, but Zenger did not.

The *Journal* criticized the governor and referred to him as a rogue, who "has nothing human but the shape." It attacked those officials who evaded the law, restricted freedom, and ruled without control. Many in New York agreed, and, as a result, the newspaper's circulation rose. The governor angrily ordered four issues of the *Journal* to be publicly burned, but the only "public" who showed up were the sheriff and his slave. The governor then ordered that Zenger be charged with seditious libel. When Zenger appeared for his bail hearing, the judge asked him how much he was worth. Zenger told him that he had no more than £40; the judge set bail at £800. His two lawyers protested, and they were disbarred. Even though a new lawyer was appointed, he offered little hope.

Suddenly, Andrew Hamilton, the most famous lawyer of his time, offered to defend Zenger. Under British law, newspapers could not print seditious libel, which was defined as articles endangering the security and peace of the state. Hamilton admitted that the *Journal* had published such articles, but if the statements were true, then the governor had not been libeled. The jury met quickly and came back with a verdict of "not guilty." A great cheer went up in the courtroom. Zenger was a free man.

RESULTS: Cosby remained in office but lost all public support. The two lawyers who had originally defended Zenger were allowed to practice law again. Zenger continued in his profession and became an official printer for the colony. Hamilton's defense was published and often praised for its defense of the public's right to be informed and to criticize bad decisions. It was a warning to royal officials that the American public was watching their performance, and even though the law was on their side, they were answerable to the public. Freedom of the press would later be protected by the First Amendment and by the public, which still sits in judgment of its governors.

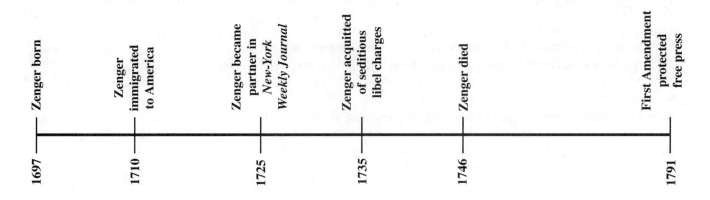

Zenger born — 1697

Zenger immigrated to America — 1710

Zenger became partner in *New-York Weekly Journal* — 1725

Zenger acquitted of seditious libel charges — 1735

Zenger died — 1746

First Amendment protected free press — 1791

Name: _____ Date: _____

The Zenger Trial and Freedom of the Press: Reinforcement

Directions: Complete the following activities, essays, and challenges on your own paper.

ACTIVITIES:

1. Look at a newspaper and find articles that would have put the editor in danger during Zenger's time.
2. Discuss the responsibility of newspapers, magazines, and television to get the facts right and not defame people.

ESSAYS:

1. Imagine that you have a corrupt mayor in your town, but you do not have a free press. How would the public know about what the mayor was doing?
2. Today movie stars get much attention from the press, some of it unfavorable. Do you think newspapers should print personal and often embarrassing details about them?
3. As a juror in the Zenger trial, explain how you decided that Zenger did not violate the law.

CHALLENGES:

1. Look up the words *libel* and *slander* in the dictionary. What is the difference between them?
2. What language did Zenger speak before he came to America?
3. Why were newspapers careful not to offend royal officials?
4. Why did lawyers have good reason to be afraid of colonial judges?
5. What is "bail"? Why did the judge set bail so high for Zenger?
6. What did the public think about Cosby and Zenger?
7. Today we elect governors and can remove them by voting them out of office, but who chose governors then?
8. What risks did Hamilton run in taking this case? Why could he succeed where the other lawyers had not?
9. What was the jury really saying when they ruled that Zenger was "not guilty"?
10. Did the fact that Zenger had been in jail ruin his career? What gives you a clue?

NATIONAL STANDARDS CORRELATIONS:

NCSS Xb: (Civic Ideals & Practice) Identify and interpret sources and examples of the rights and responsibilities of citizens.
NSH Era 2, Standard 2: How political, religious, and social institutions emerged in the English colonies

WEBSITES:

http://www.law.umkc.edu/faculty/projects/ftrials/zenger/zenger.html
"Famous American Trials: John Peter Zenger Trial, 1735," University of Missouri, Kansas City

http://jurist.law.pitt.edu/famoustrials/zenger.php
"The Trial of John Peter Zenger," University of Pittsburgh

http://earlyamerica.com/earlyamerica/bookmarks/zenger/
"Peter Zenger and Freedom of the Press," Archiving Early America

Colonists Develop a Diverse Work Force

America was a land of opportunity, without a rigid social system that made it impossible for a man to improve himself and become important. Land was available, and a hardworking person, with ambition and some luck, could rise from being a nobody to becoming an important and admired person.

Slaves Working

The vast majority of Americans were farmers, and their land had heavy forests to clear and large rocks to remove. There was hard, back-breaking work ahead in growing crops and building houses and barns. The entire family, even three-year-old children, had to do chores.

Schools were rare. Where schools existed, they could not interfere with the farm work, so they were open only one to three months during the year. The main reason for schools was to teach the student to read the Bible and to do simple math. If he wanted to go to college, a young man studied with his minister who taught him Latin and Greek. Colonists did not think it was important to educate girls, but some were taught by their fathers and brothers.

The American woman was an important part of her husband's success. She did much of the work on the farm: gardening, milking, churning butter, making clothes, and bearing children. Some had twenty or more children.

It was expected that everyone work hard, and people were judged by their financial success. If a person did not succeed in one place, then he was expected to move on to another place where he could succeed. With much work to do, Americans found the means to get more people to work for them. *Indentured servants* were brought in. These were people too poor to afford the cost of coming to America. When they arrived, they worked as servants without wages for two to seven years to pay for their transportation. Before 1776, most immigrants coming to America were indentured servants.

Apprentices were orphans or young people who had poor parents. They were sent to a master who would teach them a trade in return for their room and board. *Convict servants* would be brought in from English prisons, and their services would be sold for seven to fourteen years. Sometimes these were people who had been sentenced to prison because they couldn't pay their debts, while others were guilty of major crimes.

Slaves were brought from Africa, and they were sold to Americans. All thirteen colonies allowed slavery, but most were used in the South. In the seventeenth century, there were very few slaves; however, in the eighteenth century, many more would arrive.

RESULTS: Through various means, Americans were finding ways of building the labor force necessary to accomplish their economic goals.

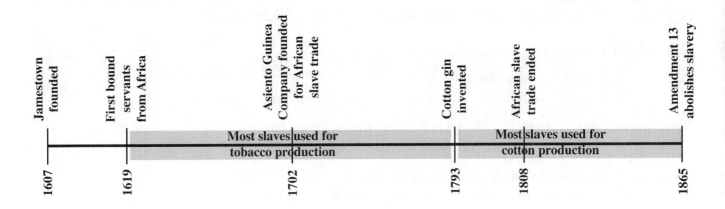

Jamestown founded	First bound servants from Africa	Asiento Guinea Company founded for African slave trade	Cotton gin invented	African slave trade ended	Amendment 13 abolishes slavery

Most slaves used for tobacco production   Most slaves used for cotton production

| 1607 | 1619 | 1702 | 1793 | 1808 | 1865 |

Name: _____ Date: _____

Colonists Develop a Diverse Work Force: Reinforcement

Directions: Complete the following activities, essays, and challenges on your own paper.

ACTIVITIES:

1. We don't use indentured servants or slaves; we have machines. Have students look around their homes for machines that save time and work. How would work have to be done if there were no blenders, electric stoves, electric irons, electric drills, etc.?
2. Discuss reasons why the ages of people getting married for the first time have changed over the years.

ESSAYS:

1. Why were women important in the colonial work force?
2. In colonial times, the measure of success was the amount of land or money the person had. How can a person today be considered successful in other things besides wealth?
3. As the son or daughter of a former indentured servant, would you be glad or unhappy that your parents came to America? Why?

CHALLENGES:

1. Why was schooling not considered as important in colonial times as it is now?
2. What term is used for a person who came willingly to America and worked without pay?
3. What term is used for a person serving a 20-year term in an English prison and who was sent to the colonies to work?
4. When a colonial man looked for a wife, what would be four qualities he might consider important?
5. When a colonial woman looked for a husband, what would be four qualities she might consider important?
6. What term was used for a 25-year-old woman who had never married?
7. What happened to orphaned children in colonial times?
8. What kinds of chores do you think a colonial boy your age would have had?
9. What kinds of chores do you think a colonial girl your age would have had?
10. What did Americans think of loafers and unsuccessful people in colonial times?

NATIONAL STANDARDS CORRELATIONS:

NCSS VIIf: (Production, Distribution, & Consumption) Explain and illustrate how values and beliefs influence different economic decisions.

NSH Era 2, Standard 1: Why the Americas attracted Europeans, why they brought enslaved Africans to their colonies, and how Europeans struggled for control of North America and the Caribbean

WEBSITES:

http://www.history.org/Almanack/life/life.cfm
"Colonial Williamsburg: Experience the Life," The Colonial Williamsburg Foundation

http://www.digitalhistory.uh.edu/black_voices/voices_display.cfm?id=14
"African-American Voices: Slavery in Colonial America," Digital History

http://www.stratfordhall.org/ed-servants.html?EDUCATION
"Indentured Servants and Transported Convicts," Stratford Hall Plantation

Washington Joins Braddock's Expedition

George Washington

England, France, and Spain were like three boxers with long memories of past battles. When they weren't fighting, they were preparing for the next match. Many who left those countries and came to America wanted to forget the past, but as long as they were colonists, they could not. They were part of a greater empire, and when rulers declared war, the shockwaves would reach them.

To the north of the British colonies was New France (Canada); French Louisiana lay west of the Mississippi River. To the south was Spain's colony, Florida. All three nations saw the importance of having Native-American allies. Algonquins supported the French, the Iroquois backed the English, and Spain's allies were the Seminoles and Creeks. When war came, the nations would recruit their Native-American allies to join their army as scouts and warriors.

In Europe, wars were fought by professional soldiers. When a king needed more trained men, he often rented them from another ruler who was not fighting. The two armies met in an open field, moved to within about fifty yards of each other, and fired volleys in unison. They did not fight in the winter or in bad weather. In America, it was much different. Battles were smaller and might be fought in any weather by untrained farmers, fur traders, fishermen, or craftsmen, under leaders they elected.

When George Washington was a boy, his older brother Lawrence taught him the basics of soldiering. George Washington became a militia officer and surveyor on the side, but most of his time was spent running the large farm he owned at Mt. Vernon on the Potomac River. Two wars had been fought in North America before Washington was born, and one ended while he was in his early teens. These involved raids on small frontier communities. Young Washington took part in the French and Indian War, which was the American part of the Seven Years' War.

The Ohio River Valley was claimed by both France and the colony of Virginia. When the governor of Virginia learned that the French were building a fort where the Ohio River formed, he sent Washington to inform them they had to leave. The French refused, so the governor sent an army under Colonel Washington to force them to leave; the army was attacked and defeated. In 1755, British soldiers led by General Edward Braddock arrived, and he recruited Virginia militia to go with his army to drive the French out. The British looked great in their red uniforms and laughed at the Americans who did not look like an army and could not march. Braddock wanted to fight as they did in Europe with the soldiers lined up in rows, marching close to each other. Washington tried to change his mind about this, but the general would not listen. When they were deep into the forest, the enemy attacked. Braddock was killed, and Washington's men covered the retreat.

RESULTS: Washington got his first battle experience and found it exciting. He also learned that fighting in America required different tactics because of its geography and its people. This war ended in 1763 with the Treaty of Paris.

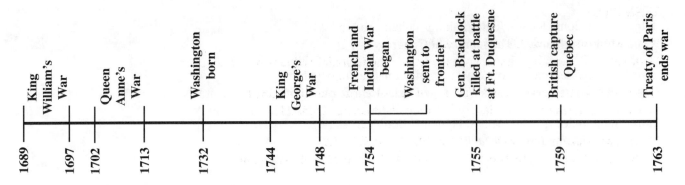

King William's War — 1689
— 1697
Queen Anne's War — 1702
— 1713
Washington born — 1732
King George's War — 1744
— 1748
French and Indian War began — 1754
Washington sent to frontier
Gen. Braddock killed at battle at Ft. Duquesne — 1755
British capture Quebec — 1759
Treaty of Paris ends war — 1763

Name: _____ Date: _____

Washington Joins Braddock's Expedition: Reinforcement

Directions: Complete the following activities, essays, and challenges on your own paper.

ACTIVITIES:

1. Research Algonquins and Iroquois on the Internet, in encyclopedias, or in other reference sources. You will learn that the beginning of the Algonquin-French relationship can be traced back to Champlain.
2. Discuss why a good system that works in one place doesn't work as well in another setting (like the European system of fighting didn't work in America).

ESSAYS:

1. As an American living in the 1750s, how would you feel when you learned that England and France were fighting a war over who would sit on the throne of Austria? Do you think we should get involved?
2. Do you think that professionals are always better than amateurs? Give arguments that could be used by both sides.
3. During the French and Indian War, Washington was in charge of protecting Virginia's frontier with 400 men. What kind of problems do you think he might have had?

CHALLENGES:

1. Who taught George Washington how to be a soldier?
2. When did the French and Indian War end?
3. How did the English feel about Algonquins? Why?
4. What were three differences between the Americans who fought in the French and Indian War and the English soldiers who served with them?
5. Look at a map and explain why the Ohio River Valley was important to both the people of Virginia and of New France.
6. Why wouldn't Braddock's tactics work in a forest?
7. Which nation owned Missouri at the beginning of the war? Which nation owned Missouri after the war?
8. Was France's colonial empire larger or smaller after the war? Why?
9. What might Washington have learned about himself from being in this battle?
10. What did Braddock write about Washington after the battle was over?

NATIONAL STANDARDS CORRELATIONS:

NCSS VIc: (Power, Authority, & Governance) Analyze and explain ideas and governmental mechanisms to meet needs and wants of citizens, regulate territory, manage conflict, and establish order and security.
NSH Era 2, Standard 1: Why the Americas attracted Europeans, why they brought enslaved Africans to their colonies, and how Europeans struggled for control of North America and the Caribbean

WEBSITES:

http://international.loc.gov/intldl/fiahtml/fiatheme3b.html
"The Military Alliance," The Library of Congress

http://www.gilderlehrman.org/teachers/boisterous/section4_4.html
"Segment 4: The Seven Years' War," The Gilder Lehrman Institute of American History

http://memory.loc.gov/ammem/today/jun04.html#necessity
"Today in History: June 4," The Library of Congress

James Otis Fights the Stamp Act

The end of the French and Indian War brought great relief to the American colonists. The French no longer threatened them from Canada. As English subjects, they were proud of their country and themselves for their role in the war. At times, English policy had bothered them. They did not like the Navigation Acts that limited their right to produce certain products and to trade with Europe and that taxed non-English imports. Since these laws had never been enforced before the war, Americans rarely thought about them.

During the war, the government tried to stop smuggling with search warrants called writs of assistance. These would allow any government official to search any home looking for anything. At that time, a Bostonian named James Otis worked for the government as a lawyer, and if anyone protested the search, it would be his job to defend the law. Rather than do that, he resigned and went to court to argue *against* the writs. He lost his case, but many Americans began to see that liberty was in danger of being lost. John Adams wrote later: "Then and there the child Independence was born."

After the Seven Years' War, England was badly in debt and felt that, since their American colonists had gained the most from the war, the colonists should pay part of the cost of sending an army to protect the frontier from Native-American attack. English leaders never considered how Americans might react. To them, Americans were like children, and the English were the parents. Anything the king and Parliament decided was something Americans must do.

In 1765, Parliament passed the Stamp Act. It required that a revenue stamp be placed on legal documents, newspapers, and marriage licenses. They also passed the Quartering Act, which said Americans would have to provide housing for 10,000 British soldiers who would be sent to protect them. The Americans did not like taxes, and they did not want the soldiers.

Again, Otis was on his feet complaining, but this time, others were with him. Patrick Henry told the Virginia legislature that Americans had every right that Englishmen had, and one of the most important English rights was that citizens could not be taxed without representation. He said the only people who could tax in their colony were Virginians.

In the Massachusetts legislature, Otis called for a meeting of the Colonies to take place in October 1765. Nine colonies sent delegates to the meeting. They said they were loyal to the king, and admitted that Parliament had the right to pass laws for the Colonies. However, they stated that only the colonial legislature could tax the people. On the streets, groups of men and boys calling themselves Sons of Liberty destroyed stamps and threatened those who had been appointed as stamp agents.

RESULTS: American protests and a change of leadership in Parliament caused the Stamp Act to be repealed. Americans cheered when they heard the good news. They paid no attention to a law called the Declaratory Act passed at the same time, which said that England had every right to make any law for the Colonies that they chose. This would lead to future trouble.

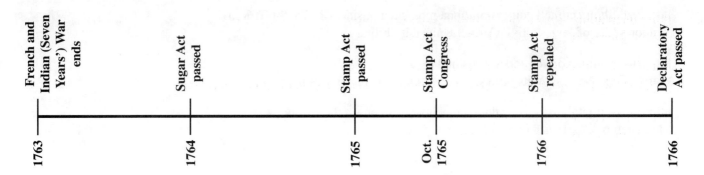

French and Indian (Seven Years') War ends	Sugar Act passed	Stamp Act passed	Stamp Act Congress	Stamp Act repealed	Declaratory Act passed
1763	1764	1765	Oct. 1765	1766	1766

Name: _____ Date: _____

James Otis Fights the Stamp Act: Reinforcement

Directions: Complete the following activities, essays, and challenges on your own paper.

ACTIVITIES:

1. Americans were angered over a small tax on newspapers, etc. Make a list of the taxes we pay now.
2. A friend of yours is interested in becoming a stamp tax agent in 1765. How would the class try to dissuade him?

ESSAYS:

1. What does the phrase "A man's home is his castle" mean? What would be the effect of writs of assistance on that principle?
2. Many Americans, including Ben Franklin, were surprised by the violence that occurred in Boston when stamps were burned and the property of the men who were going to sell the stamps was destroyed. As a person living in Boston at the time, would you have felt those who were responsible for this destruction were out of line?
3. Amendment III of the U.S. Constitution says, "No Soldier shall, in time of peace, be quartered in any house, without the consent of the Owner, nor in time of war, but in a manner to be prescribed by law." Why did Americans consider this a right that needed to be guaranteed in the Bill of Rights?

CHALLENGES:

1. How many British soldiers did the king plan to send to America?
2. What did James Otis do for a living?
3. Why didn't Americans protest the Navigation Acts?
4. What did the king and other English leaders think about Americans?
5. Look in a dictionary to see how it describes a search warrant. What is its purpose?
6. Why might a writ of assistance cause problems for a person who spoke up against the government?
7. Why were Americans so upset over the Stamp Act?
8. How did Americans feel when the Stamp Act was repealed?
9. Why did Parliament pass the Declaratory Act?
10. Did Americans want war with England in 1765? What makes you think so?

NATIONAL STANDARDS CORRELATIONS:

NCSS VIb: (Power, Authority, & Governance) Describe the purpose of government and how its powers are acquired, used, and justified.
NSH Era 3, Standard 1: The causes of the American Revolution, the ideas and interests involved in forging the revolutionary movement, and the reasons for the American victory

WEBSITES:

http://cdl.library.cornell.edu/cgi-bin/moa/moa-cgi?notisid=ABQ7578-0016-25
"Tudor's Life of James Otis," Cornell University Library

http://www.nhinet.org/ccs/docs/writs.htm
"James Otis: Against Writs of Assistance," National Humanities Institute

http://www.digital history.uh.edu/documents/documents_p2.cfm?doc=258
"The Stamp Act Crisis," Digital History

Sam Adams' Tea Party

After the Stamp Act controversy, relations with England never got back to normal. In 1766, Charles Townshend became Chancellor of the Exchequer (treasurer) of England. The next year, he persuaded Parliament to levy a tax on American imports of lead, paper, glass, and tea. Money from the tax would pay the salaries of British officials in America. In the past, legislatures had paid their salaries and used paychecks as a way to control the governors. Americans protested again and stopped buying British goods (a boycott). The men chosen as tax collectors knew they were unpopular, and those in Boston were protected by two regiments of Redcoats (British soldiers). Redcoats on American soil were unpopular, and Sam Adams used that to turn molehills into mountains. He would not rest until America was independent, and there were neither British soldiers nor officials on American soil.

Sam Adams

Adams was a strange man. He was a Harvard graduate, smart in studies, but terrible in business. He took over his father's business, and it went broke. He became Boston's tax collector and didn't collect the taxes. By the time he was 42 years old, his hair was gray, and his hands shook when he spoke; he dressed poorly and had very little money. There was one thing he did well—he stirred up the public. Since he was poor, he needed and got the financial support of the wealthy shipowner John Hancock. When James Otis developed a mental illness, Adams replaced him as the anti-British leader.

In 1770, a British soldier on guard duty was pelted with snowballs, and other British soldiers came to his rescue. A mob gathered around them; one soldier was knocked down and another hit with a cane. The soldiers fired and killed four civilians. Sam Adams called it the "Boston Massacre" and persuaded a silversmith, Paul Revere, to make an engraving of it so people could not only read about it but see it.

The American boycott was successful, and Parliament once again backed down, but not completely. Rather than remove all the Townshend duties, they kept the tax on tea. The only legal tea was that imported by the East India Company; however, it sold directly to the customer. American merchants who sold smuggled tea did not like that and stirred opposition to the tea tax as a way to get public support behind them.

When Sam Adams learned that tea ships had arrived in Boston, he organized an unusual protest. He and his friends dressed in costumes like Mohawks and dumped 342 chests of tea into the harbor. Some Americans approved of this, but others, like Benjamin Franklin and George Washington, did not. If England had not reacted as it did, it would have been a soon-forgotten act of vandalism, but George III made it an important event.

RESULTS: The English overreacted and passed a series of laws known in America as the Intolerable Acts (Coercive Acts in England). They closed the port of Boston, put Massachusetts under a military governor, and housed troops in private homes. Americans would unite as never before against these laws. If England could treat one colony that way, all were in danger of losing their freedom.

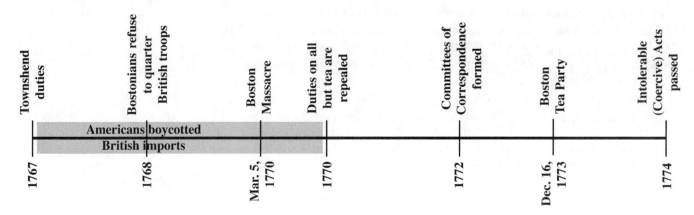

Townshend duties — 1767

Bostonians refuse to quarter British troops — 1768

Americans boycotted British imports

Boston Massacre — Mar. 5, 1770

Duties on all but tea are repealed — 1770

Committees of Correspondence formed — 1772

Boston Tea Party — Dec. 16, 1773

Intolerable (Coercive) Acts passed — 1774

Name: _____ Date: _____

Sam Adams' Tea Party: Reinforcement

Directions: Complete the following activities, essays, and challenges on your own paper.

ACTIVITIES:

1. Propaganda techniques are often used in modern politics. Discuss some techniques that are used by politicians and advertisers.
2. Apply the Intolerable Acts to the punishment of a state. Discuss how it would affect your state.

ESSAYS:

1. Why did Americans use boycotts as a way to protest? What does it take for a boycott to be effective?
2. After reading a biography of Sam Adams, what do you think about him?
3. If you were Sam Adams, would you be pleased with the passing of the Coercive Acts? Why or why not?

CHALLENGES:

1. What four items did Townshend want to tax?
2. Why did Americans want to pay royal governors out of their own pockets?
3. What was a Redcoat? Why were they unpopular?
4. What is meant by "turning molehills into mountains"? How might you use that phrase to discuss someone you know?
5. Why would a boycott hurt English merchants?
6. Why did Sam Adams need Hancock?
7. What caused the "Boston Massacre"? What else could it have been called?
8. What was Paul Revere's role in making the Boston Massacre famous?
9. What company sold the only legal tea to Americans?
10. Define the word *intolerable*. Why would Americans use that term to describe the Coercive Acts?

NATIONAL STANDARDS CORRELATIONS:

NCSS Xf: (Civic Ideals & Practices) Identify and explain the roles of formal and informal political actors in influencing and shaping public policy and decision-making.
NSH Era 3, Standard 1: The causes of the American Revolution, the ideas and interests involved in forging the revolutionary movement, and the reasons for the American victory

WEBSITES:

http://www.digitalhistory.uh.edu/documents/documents_p2.cfm?doc=252
"The Boston Tea Party," Digital History

http://www.whitehouse.gov/kids/dreamteam/samueladams.html
"White House Dream Team: Samuel Adams," The White House

http://www.digitalhistory.uh.edu/document/documents_p2.cfm?doc=281
"The Townsend Acts," Digital History

http://www.memory.loc.gov/ammem/bdsds/timeline.html
"Time Line, America During the Age of Revolution, 1764–1775," The Library of Congress

Patrick Henry Demands Liberty or Death

Patrick Henry

Americans were outraged when they learned Parliament had passed the Intolerable Acts. It was unreasonable that a whole colony be punished for the actions of a few men. If England could do this to Massachusetts, what would prevent the same thing happening to any other colony that offended the king? Protest was heard now in other parts of British America, but the most eloquent was by Virginia's Patrick Henry.

The son of a tobacco farmer, Patrick Henry hated farm work as a boy, so his father gave him a store to run—it lost money. He got married at an early age, and his parents gave the new couple a farm, but the house burned. He tried running a store again, but once more he failed. He had made some progress, though; he had learned to enjoy reading and decided to become a lawyer. He barely made it past the bar examination, but he was popular and soon had a thriving law practice. In 1763, he took a case involving a minister's pay and turned it into an attack on the king. His opposition called this treason, but the audience was in his hands.

In 1765, he was elected to Virginia's House of Burgesses. This was the year of the Stamp Act, and no one doubted his opinion on that subject. He pushed five resolutions through the House protesting this violation of the English constitution. When that issue passed, he turned away from public issues to his law practice for a time. In 1774 when word reached Virginia of the Intolerable Acts, Henry could not sit idly by while freedom was in danger. He was pleased to be chosen as a member of the First Continental Congress, which met in Philadelphia.

Most delegates were not as outspoken against England as were Sam Adams and Patrick Henry. Adams had been advised not to mention the word "independence," for fear it would only scare off Southern delegates, so he sat quietly and let Patrick Henry do the speaking. Henry proclaimed, "The distinctions between Virginians, Pennsylvanians, New Yorkers, and New Englanders are no more. I am not a Virginian, but an American." A resolution was passed declaring the Coercive Acts unconstitutional, but there was no demand for independence.

When General Thomas Gage arrived in Boston with an army, Governor Dunmore of Virginia feared the worst from men like Henry and barred the doors to the House of Burgesses. The legislators met in Richmond, and Henry gave his most famous speech. He said the time for patience was over, that every effort to persuade the king had failed, and closed with, "Is life so dear or peace so sweet as to be purchased at the price of chains and slavery? Forbid it, Almighty God. I know not what course others may take, but as for me, give me liberty or give me death!"

RESULTS: Henry's words had a force to them that still affects people who feel their liberty is endangered. The memory of those words was to become useful in 1776, when debate began on whether or not to declare independence.

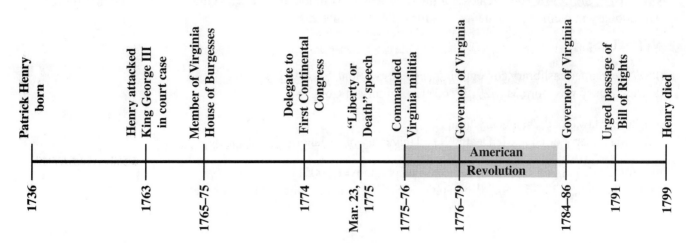

Name: _____ Date: _____

Patrick Henry Demands Liberty or Death: Reinforcement

Directions: Complete the following activities, essays, and challenges on your own paper.

ACTIVITIES:

1. What makes a good orator? Have students listen to a recording of a famous speaker like Franklin D. Roosevelt, Winston Churchill, or John F. Kennedy.
2. Considering the mood of the times, discuss Governor Dunmore's handling of the situation and whether he could have gotten better results with a different approach.

ESSAYS:

1. Patrick Henry said, "Give me liberty or give me death!" Why would a person prefer to die if he could not be free? Would you feel the same way?
2. After reading about Sam Adams and Patrick Henry, discuss how they were alike and how they were different.
3. Moses Tyler wrote that Patrick Henry saw virtue, morality, and religion as the armor that made America invincible (undefeatable). What do you see as America's strengths?

CHALLENGES:

1. What was Patrick Henry's first job, and how did he like it?
2. Why were people in Virginia upset over a problem in New England?
3. Why was Sam Adams so quiet during the First Continental Congress?
4. When was the earliest time mentioned in this reading that Henry spoke out against the British government?
5. How much preparation did a person have to go through to become a lawyer in those days?
6. What was the lower House of the Virginia legislature called?
7. What was Governor Dunmore worried about, and what did he do?
8. What was the big "I" word that delegates didn't want to use in 1774?
9. What did Patrick Henry mean by: "I am not a Virginian, but an American"?
10. "Give me liberty or give me death!" is a very famous statement. What other statements of that type can you recall?

NATIONAL STANDARDS CORRELATIONS:

<u>NCSS Xf:</u> (Civic Ideals & Practices) Identify and explain the roles of formal and informal political actors in influencing and shaping public policy and decision making.
<u>NSH Era 3, Standard 1:</u> The causes of the American Revolution, the ideas and interests involved in forging the revolutionary movement, and the reasons for the American victory

WEBSITES:

http://www.americaslibrary.gov/cgi-bin/page.cgi/jb/colonial/henry_1
"Patrick Henry was Born May 29, 1736," The Library of Congress

http://www.law.ou.edu/hist/henry/html
"Give Me Liberty or Give Me Death," The University of Oklahoma Law Center

http://bioguide.congress.gov/scripts/biodisplay.pl?index=H000511
"Henry, Patrick, (1736–1799)," Biographical Directory of the United States Congress

The Declaration of Independence Is Signed

Events moved swiftly after General Thomas Gage arrived in Boston. Some Americans, who wanted to be loyal to England but wanted to have more freedom, came up with ideas for developing a dominion status. That is, Parliament would have no control over them, but they would stay loyal to the king. People like Sam Adams and Patrick Henry did not like that idea. When the demands of Congress that British troops be withdrawn reached the king, he and Parliament agreed that Massachusetts was in a state of rebellion.

The king's troops ruled in Boston, but outside the city it was the Committee of Safety that was in charge. They were gathering guns and gunpowder, drilling their militia, and preparing for a showdown. Gage's spies told him about arms being collected at Lexington and Concord, Massachusetts, and he sent approximately 700 men to destroy the supplies. Paul Revere and William Dawes rode to warn the Americans that the British were coming. Dawes escaped British patrols, but Revere was captured and held for a time.

At Lexington and again at Concord, the militia faced the British, and after someone fired (no one is sure which side fired first), British volleys forced the inexperienced militia to leave in a hurry. The British soldiers found little in the way of ammunition or supplies to take, so they marched back to Boston. Americans attacked them all the way, and the British casualties included 73 men killed, 174 wounded.

Richard Henry Lee

Americans led by Ethan Allen and Benedict Arnold captured Ft. Ticonderoga on Lake Champlain, capturing the 42 soldiers stationed there. Tensions ran high in Boston, which was now surrounded by militia. With all of these events occurring, sessions of the Second Continental Congress were tense. The decision to appoint George Washington to command the army was a big step toward separation, but delegates were still reluctant to face the big question, which was: "Are the thirteen English colonies in North America prepared to break their historic ties to the greatest empire on earth?" From that question came others. If we do try, can we win? Who might we persuade to help us? What will happen to those who sign a document declaring independence if the effort fails? The only question for which they knew the answer was the last. If they failed, the penalty for traitors included hanging (but not until dead), heads cut off, and bodies divided into quarters.

In June 1776, Richard Henry Lee of Virginia proposed, "That these united colonies are, and of right ought to be, free and independent states." This caused much debate, and many members had to wait for instructions from home before they could vote. A committee was formed to draft a formal document explaining to the world the reasons for their actions. The committee included John Adams, Benjamin Franklin, and Thomas Jefferson. The others left Jefferson with the job of writing the Declaration of Independence.

RESULTS: The document was approved on July 4, 1776. As Benjamin Franklin stood in line to sign it, he commented, "We must all hang together, or assuredly we shall all hang separately." It was meant as humor, but there was a truth to it that the others all understood. To fail was to die, but honor and liberty were worth the risk.

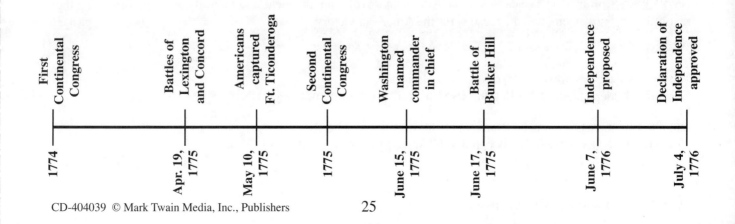

First Continental Congress — 1774

Battles of Lexington and Concord — Apr. 19, 1775

Americans captured Ft. Ticonderoga — May 10, 1775

Second Continental Congress — 1775

Washington named commander in chief — June 15, 1775

Battle of Bunker Hill — June 17, 1775

Independence proposed — June 7, 1776

Declaration of Independence approved — July 4, 1776

Name: _____ Date: _____

The Declaration of Independence Is Signed: Reinforcement

Directions: Complete the following activities, essays, and challenges on your own paper.

ACTIVITIES:

1. Have students read the Declaration of Independence aloud and listen for important quotes. Instruct them to rewrite the first paragraph in their own words.
2. Have students tell how they would feel if they were asked to sign a statement to always do their best work, and that if they did not, the government would put them in jail. That should give them some of the same thoughts that the signers of the Declaration of Independence had.

ESSAYS:

1. Benjamin Franklin said, "We must all hang together, or assuredly we shall all hang separately." As a person standing in line to sign the document, what would that remark mean to you?
2. Read the Declaration of Independence and look for important phrases. Rewrite them in your own words.
3. Someone in your class argues that the war had begun before the Declaration of Independence was signed. Would you agree or disagree? Why?

CHALLENGES:

1. What is meant by a "dominion"?
2. Why would Sam Adams or Patrick Henry oppose being a dominion?
3. What two men warned the people that the British were coming? Which of them became the most famous? Why?
4. Why did General Gage send troops to Lexington and Concord? Was what he found worth the trip?
5. Where is Lake Champlain located?
6. Why was the selection of Washington as commander of the army an important step toward independence?
7. Who proposed that the Colonies declare independence?
8. One of Benjamin Franklin's most famous quotations is in this selection. What other Benjamin Franklin quotes do you know? List one.
9. Three members of the Second Continental Congress appointed to draft a Declaration of Independence were John Adams (1735–1826), Ben Franklin (1706–1790), and Thomas Jefferson (1743–1826). Of the three, who was oldest? Which of the three men had the longest life? Which had a cousin who was a strong supporter for independence? Which man was 33 years old when the Declaration of Independence was signed?
10. What would have happened to those who signed the Declaration if the war for independence had failed?

NATIONAL STANDARDS CORRELATIONS:

NCSS VIb: (Power, Authority, & Governance) Describe the purpose of government and how its powers are acquired, used, and justified.
NSH Era 3, Standard 1: The causes of the American Revolution, the ideas and interests involved in forging the revolutionary movement, and the reasons for the American victory

WEBSITES:

http://www.loc.gov/exhibits/declara/declara3.html
"Declaring Independence: Drafting the Documents," The Library of Congress

http://www.usconstitution.net/declarsigndata.html
"Signers of the Declaration of Independence," Steve Mount

Washington Stages a Surprise Attack on Trenton

General William Howe

As Washington rode to Boston to take command of his army, a messenger informed him that a battle had taken place, known today as the Battle of Bunker Hill. General Gage had sent General William Howe's British soldiers to take the hill held by the militia. Three attempts were made before the Americans withdrew, but one-third of Howe's men were dead or wounded. Howe had expected an easy win, but the results shocked him. He was more careful after that.

When the guns captured at Ft. Ticonderoga arrived, American militia put them into place on the hills overlooking Boston harbor. Gage ordered the British navy to take the army to Nova Scotia. This gave Washington time to organize his army. In battle, he would depend on the men recruited by Congress, the Continentals. They would be his "professionals." Since each colony had its own militia, he would use them as well, but he always feared they could not stand the pressure of battle. His officers were chosen by Congress, many for political reasons. His main problem was not the English army but getting the supplies he needed. The French secretly sent the Americans guns and ammunition, but there were other shortages as well: food, clothing, shelter, and pay for the men. Many soldiers deserted; Thomas Paine called them "sunshine patriots." Washington guessed that when the British returned from Canada, their target would be New York City. He put some men on Long Island, the others on Manhattan.

Washington guessed right; General Howe landed on Long Island with 32,000 men, including 9,000 German professional soldiers. Since most of these were from Hesse, Americans called all the German soldiers Hessians. At Long Island, the Americans did not fight well, but a heavy rain came, so Washington was able to withdraw to Manhattan. While there, he was defeated again. His men dropped their guns and ran from the oncoming British soldiers. He tried to turn them around, and when he finally realized they were gone, he sat on his horse, practically begging the British to kill him on the spot. One of his officers came back and led the horse away. Howe did not finish the job that night. While British soldiers slept, a heavy fog descended, and Washington's men escaped again.

The British spent the winter with their army scattered in New York and New Jersey. So far, they had won all the battles, but Washington was still loose and dangerous. Knowing that German troops were at Trenton and were surely not expecting an attack in a snowstorm on Christmas Day, Washington's men crossed the Delaware River. The German colonel was warned of a possible attack, but the note was in English, and he couldn't read English, so he just put it inside his coat. The battle was swift, and 1,400 Germans were either killed or captured. Later, the note was read to the dying colonel.

RESULTS: Trenton was one among many battles, but it gave confidence to an army that had been trounced time after time. Many soldiers who had planned to leave, stayed. New men joined the army. For Washington, it was the beginning of a brighter day.

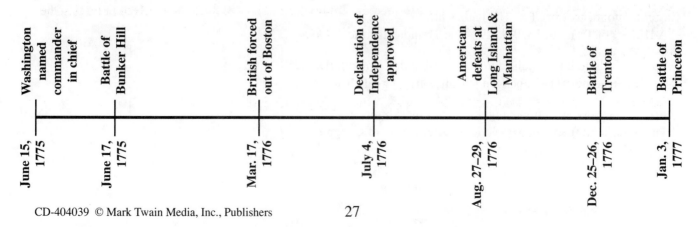

Washington named commander in chief	Battle of Bunker Hill	British forced out of Boston	Declaration of Independence approved	American defeats at Long Island & Manhattan	Battle of Trenton	Battle of Princeton
June 15, 1775	June 17, 1775	Mar. 17, 1776	July 4, 1776	Aug. 27–29, 1776	Dec. 25–26, 1776	Jan. 3, 1777

Name: _____ Date: _____

Washington Stages a Surprise Attack on Trenton: Reinforcement

Directions: Complete the following activities, essays, and challenges on your own paper.

ACTIVITIES:

1. Use a map to locate some of the places mentioned in the reading selection. Discuss the difficulties moving an army 50 miles through a blizzard and across an icy river without enough clothes to keep warm.
2. Discuss the "sunshine patriot." How does that apply to your school's competitive teams?

ESSAYS:

1. If you were a German soldier who had been "rented out" by your ruler, how hard would you fight in this war in North America? Why?
2. Howe's nickname for Washington was the "Grey Fox." Remembering that in that time, foxes were hunted by the hounds, how would Howe feel about his image of Washington after this?
3. As a signer of the Declaration of Independence, you have received word of the victory at Trenton. You write a letter to General Washington. What would you say?

CHALLENGES:

1. What British general captured Bunker Hill? How did he feel about his victory?
2. Why did Gage leave Boston?
3. Who were the Continentals?
4. What do you think Paine meant by "sunshine patriots"?
5. The Americans felt that God had spared them after the battles at Long Island and Manhattan. Why do you suppose they thought that?
6. How did Washington react to the way his men handled themselves at Manhattan? Have you ever seen a coach act that way?
7. How did the fact that the commander at Trenton was German help Washington?
8. What problems made the attack especially hard for Washington's men?
9. How many Germans were either killed or captured that day?
10. How did Washington's troops react to the victory?

NATIONAL STANDARDS CORRELATIONS:

NCSS VId: (Power, Authority, & Governance) Describe the ways nations and organizations respond to forces of unity and diversity affecting order and security.
NSH Era 3, Standard 1: The causes of the American Revolution, the ideas and interests involved in forging the revolutionary movement, and the reasons for the American victory

WEBSITES:

http://trentonhistory.org/Exp/His/battles.htm
"A History of Trenton, 1679–1929," The Trenton Historical Society

http://www.digitalhistory.uh.edu/database/subtitles.cfm?titleID=53
"Guided Readings: The American Revolution," Digital History

http://memory.loc.gov/ammem/gwhtml/gwtimear.html
"Timeline: The American Revolution," The Library of Congress

Saratoga: Little People Mess Up Grand Plans

In charge of British grand strategy during the war was George Germain, the Colonial Secretary. A former general, he had turned to politics and was a backer of Prime Minister Lord North. There were many problems in getting anything done: (1) It took months for orders to reach America; by the time they arrived, the situation had changed. Officers did not have to obey orders that did not fit the current situation. (2) Supplies were slowed down by storms or calms at sea. (3) Morale was low in the English army. Many of the best British generals refused to fight the Americans. (4) Washington and his Patriot troops were stubborn; no other army marched without shoes or food. (5) Battles might be lost because of odd occurrences.

General John Burgoyne

In 1777, Germain sent instructions for a campaign that would cut New England off from the Middle Colonies and split New York. General William Howe would start up the Hudson Valley from New York; General Barry St. Leger would invade western New York and move down the Mohawk Valley to the Hudson River. General John Burgoyne would come down Lake Champlain and the Hudson Valley and join the other forces at Albany. However, decisions were made that made a shamble of the plans.

General Howe's girlfriend thought New York was dull and that the best parties were in Philadelphia. She convinced Howe that since Philadelphia was the rebel capital, he should move his army there, so instead of going north, he moved to Philadelphia, which offered no support for the other two armies.

St. Leger was a capable young officer whose troops landed at Oswego, New York, and moved toward Ft. Stanwix, which he surrounded with a force of English and Native Americans. A messenger escaped and told American General Benedict Arnold. He formed a small army and started toward Ft. Stanwix. On the way, he met a boy named Hon Yost, whose brother was held as a British spy and was about to be shot. Arnold and Yost made a deal: Yost could save his brother's life by running into the Native-American camp and telling them about the huge American army that was coming. Some holes were shot in Yost's coat to make the story look good. He did such a good job of describing the American approach that the Native Americans left and so did St. Leger.

Meanwhile, Burgoyne was making a leisurely trip out of his march. His slow march gave time for the story of Jenny McCrae to spread. Jenny, whose fiancé was a young British officer, decided to travel north to meet him. She was killed and scalped by two Native-American scouts of Burgoyne's army. When Jenny's fiancé saw her long red hair hanging from the scouts' scalplocks, he demanded that the scouts be punished. But Burgoyne feared that if he punished these Native Americans, the others would desert, so he did nothing. The story of Jenny McCrae was told many times, and many men joined General Horatio Gates' Patriot army. Surrounded by this larger force, Burgoyne surrendered his 5,000 men to the Americans.

RESULTS: Many things happened because of Saratoga. Morale in England dropped, and many wanted to end the war. The French decided that the Americans could win and made an alliance.

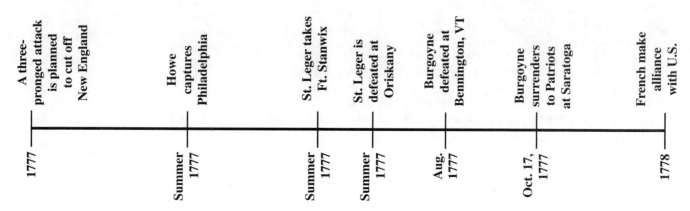

A three-pronged attack is planned to cut off New England	Howe captures Philadelphia	St. Leger takes Ft. Stanwix	St. Leger is defeated at Oriskany	Burgoyne defeated at Bennington, VT	Burgoyne surrenders to Patriots at Saratoga	French make alliance with U.S.
1777	Summer 1777	Summer 1777	Summer 1777	Aug. 1777	Oct. 17, 1777	1778

Name: _____ Date: _____

Saratoga: Little People Mess Up Grand Plans: Reinforcement

Directions: Complete the following activities, essays, and challenges on your own paper.

ACTIVITIES:

1. Discuss how individuals can alter the affairs of a town or country for the better or for the worse.
2. Discuss the influence of an event (like the murder of Jenny McCrae) in causing people who have done little to suddenly react.

ESSAYS:

1. A turning point is one that causes one side to lose the ability or the will to win. Why could that term be used to describe Saratoga?
2. Germain's grand plan fell apart. What are the advantages and disadvantages of grand plans?
3. Germain got his job through political ties with the prime minister. What advice might you give an official who was choosing a friend for a high position after learning about Germain?

CHALLENGES:

1. What 15-year-old boy messed up St. Leger's plan? How did he do it?
2. What position did George Germain hold?
3. You are a British soldier in 1777. Under which commander would you have served if you had been at Ft. Stanwix?
4. Under which British commander would you have served if you had been at Saratoga?
5. Under which British commander would you have served if you had been in Philadelphia?
6. What color hair did Jenny McCrae have? Why was that important?
7. How did General Howe's girlfriend persuade him that taking Philadelphia was more important than violating orders?
8. What general took credit for the battle at Saratoga?
9. What is a siege? How can you win in a siege without firing a shot?
10. What is morale? Why is it important?

NATIONAL STANDARDS CORRELATIONS:

NCSS VId: (Power, Authority, & Governance) Describe the ways nations and organizations respond to forces of unity and diversity affecting order and security.
NSH Era 3, Standard 1: The causes of the American Revolution, the ideas and interests involved in forging the revolutionary movement, and the reasons for the American victory

WEBSITES:

http://www.nps.gov/sara/s-batles.htm
"Story of the Battles," National Park Service

http://www.pbs.org/ktca/liberty/chronicle_saratoga1777.html
"Liberty: The American Revolution," Public Broadcasting Service

http://earlyamerica.com/earlyamerica/maps/saratogamap/
"A Map Showing the Position of General Burgoyne's Army at the Battle of Saratoga on Oct. 10, 1777," Archiving Early America

Benedict Arnold Betrays the Cause

Benedict Arnold

From Ft. Ticonderoga on, Benedict Arnold's name was listed among the most outstanding American officers, and he had earned the trust of General Washington. Pride and a desire for wealth eventually won over loyalty.

Arnold's father was the town drunk, and his mother was a stern woman. Tired of taking orders from her, he joined the militia during the French and Indian War. At 21, he went to New Haven, Connecticut, and became a book salesman and pharmacist. When he learned of the Battle at Lexington, he got a colonel's commission, and together with Ethan Allen's Green Mountain Boys, took Ft. Ticonderoga and its guns. When he returned, he learned that his wife had died, and Congress would pay only a fraction of his expenses.

He joined General Richard Montgomery's unsuccessful expedition to capture Quebec and received a bad leg wound during the attempt. When General Guy Carleton's English troops tried to move down Lake Champlain in 1776, Arnold blocked them. He was given the rank of brigadier general, but Congress criticized the fact that his books were not in order. The next February, five brigadiers were raised to major generals, but he was passed over. Washington demanded an explanation and was told that Connecticut already had two major generals.

Washington persuaded Arnold to stay in the army. After he played a major role in stopping St. Leger's drive down the Mohawk Valley, Arnold joined Gates' army at Saratoga. In the battle, Arnold led charges against Burgoyne's lines and received a thigh wound. Envious of Arnold's standing with Washington, Gates did not mention Arnold in his official report of the battle.

While Arnold was recovering from his wounds, Washington put him in charge at Philadelphia, where he fell in love with and married an English sympathizer, Peggy Shippen. Peggy had more expensive tastes than he could afford, and he fell heavily into debt. In addition, Pennsylvania officials charged that he was using their militia as his personal servants. It was not hard for Arnold to excuse what he and Peggy now planned.

Secret discussions were held with British agents. Arnold was to persuade Washington to give him command at West Point, an important position on the Hudson River, and then he would turn it over to the British. Washington was surprised when Arnold asked for West Point, but gave in to his friend's request. Once at West Point, contact was made with a British spy, Major John Andre. They agreed that if Arnold could deliver West Point, he would receive £20,000 and a brigadier general's commission. On his way south after the meeting, Andre was captured, and the secret papers were found inside his shoe. Arnold made a quick getaway, just before Washington arrived on an inspection tour.

RESULTS: When Washington was given evidence of what Arnold had done, he could hardly believe it at first, but he sent his men out to find him. Arnold was next seen leading Loyalist troops, and he escaped to England when the British army surrendered. His reputation was ruined; the British, like the Americans, saw him only as a traitor.

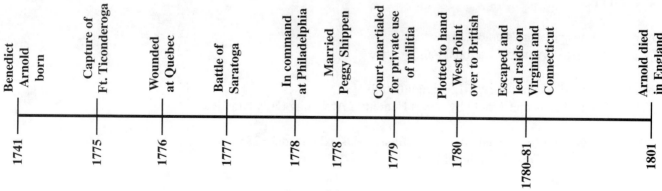

1741	1775	1776	1777	1778	1778	1779	1780	1780–81	1801
Benedict Arnold born	Capture of Ft. Ticonderoga	Wounded at Quebec	Battle of Saratoga	In command at Philadelphia	Married Peggy Shippen	Court-martialed for private use of militia	Plotted to hand West Point over to British	Escaped and led raids on Virginia and Connecticut	Arnold died in England

Name: _____ Date: _____

Benedict Arnold Betrays the Cause: Reinforcement

Directions: Complete the following activities, essays, and challenges on your own paper.

ACTIVITIES:

1. The term "Benedict Arnold" is used today to describe a traitor. Discuss whether the class thinks that is fair, in light of all he did for the Revolution.
2. When the Constitution was written, the only crime it specifically stressed was treason and the punishment for treason (Article III, Section 3). Ask the class why they think treason is regarded as such a terrible crime.

ESSAYS:

1. Do you think that Arnold was a hero, a coward, a confused man, or something else? Why?
2. You are Benedict Arnold, and you write a former army friend after the war. How would you explain your actions?
3. General Washington considered the betrayal by Arnold as his worst experience of the war. Write what you think the general might have said in his diary after he learned what had happened.

CHALLENGES:

1. What civilian jobs did Arnold have?
2. In what war did he have his first military experience?
3. How many times was he wounded in battle? In what parts of his body?
4. Who led the expedition against Quebec on which Arnold went?
5. What British general did he stop on Lake Champlain in 1776?
6. What caused Arnold to fall so heavily into debt?
7. What British spy contacted Arnold?
8. How many pounds (£) did Arnold receive for his treachery?
9. Why is the fort he tried to betray important today?
10. How was Arnold treated by the British after the war?

NATIONAL STANDARDS CORRELATIONS:

NCSS Xf: (Civic Ideals & Practices) Identify and explain the roles of formal and informal political actors in influencing and shaping public policy and decision-making.
NSH Era 3, Standard 1: The cause of the American Revolution, the ideas and interests involved in forging the revolutionary movement, and the reasons for the American victory

WEBSITES:

http://www.nps.gov/sara/s-arnold.htm
"General Benedict Arnold," National Park Service

http://earlyamerica.com/review/fall97/arnold.html
"The Enigma of Benedict Arnold by James Henretta," Archiving Early America

http://www.digitalhistory.uh.edu/documents/doucments_p2.cfm?doc=283
"Benedict Arnold's Treason," Digital History

A Peace Treaty Is Made With England in 1783

Benjamin Franklin

A basic part of the colonists' strategy from the beginning of the war had been to win European support. America would need guns, gunpowder, and financial support. Since England had humiliated the Spanish in 1588, and the French in 1763, those countries naturally disliked them. Holland was a rival on the oceans and would also like England put in its place. The United States sent diplomats to Europe to encourage them to help. Ben Franklin was the key diplomat in France, John Jay in Spain, and John Adams in Holland. Of these, the best-known was Franklin.

Noted for his scientific discoveries, his inventions, and his words of wisdom in *Poor Richard's Almanack,* the French public adored Ben Franklin. Since they saw Americans as backwoodsmen, Franklin started wearing a coonskin cap. Beyond the showmanship, there was purpose behind his actions. He got secret shipments of supplies, he talked to young officers eager to volunteer for the American army, and he arranged for the French to give secret grants and loans. At first, Count Vergennes, the French foreign minister, dared not give open support to the Americans; they might quit fighting, and England would have every excuse to pounce on France.

The victory at Saratoga caused Vergennes to push the reluctant King Louis XVI to recognize the United States. Two treaties were signed; the first was a trade treaty, and the second was an alliance. Each side promised it would continue to fight until the war was won; neither would stop fighting without getting the permission of the other.

The war was far from over when the agreements were signed, but English hopes were clearly fading. England was even offering self-rule within the British empire. Their agents tried to bribe members of Congress and Franklin to get them to agree to sell out the cause. When British agents approached Franklin, he told them the only terms acceptable would be: independence, British troops must leave American soil, and America would gain the right to fish off the Great Bank of Newfoundland. Franklin called in Jay and Adams to help with the work. Jay did not trust the French to put American interests above those of France. He suggested America make its own deal with England. Adams agreed with Jay, and the outnumbered Franklin gave in. A preliminary Treaty of Peace was signed in 1782.

The problem was the Americans had violated their agreement with France, and neither side would stop fighting without the consent of the other. Ben Franklin was chosen to write the letter to Vergennes telling him what America had done. He explained that this was only a "preliminary" treaty and would not be binding until after France approved. In 1783, the Treaty of Paris was signed. It gave America independence and the region west to the Mississippi River. Florida was given back to Spain. Congress was to ask states to return the property of Loyalists (those supporting England) that had been seized by the states.

RESULTS: The colonial period was over. The United States of America was a proud new independent nation, but was it a nation or thirteen independent states each moving in its own direction? Only the future would tell.

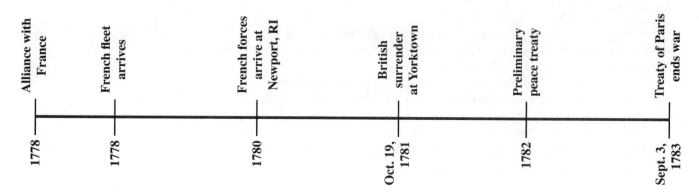

Alliance with France	French fleet arrives	French forces arrive at Newport, RI	British surrender at Yorktown	Preliminary peace treaty	Treaty of Paris ends war
1778	1778	1780	Oct. 19, 1781	1782	Sept. 3, 1783

Name: _____ Date: _____

A Peace Treaty Is Made With England in 1783: Reinforcement

Directions: Complete the following activities, essays, and challenges on your own paper.

ACTIVITIES:

1. Discuss the peace treaty and its terms. Note that Americans would have accepted the treaty if it had just included the region east of the Appalachians, but the English gave more to break up the American-French team.
2. Discuss why diplomats must always be on guard in dealing with other nations. Remember that a diplomat puts his country's interests first.

ESSAYS:

1. A diplomat's job is not easy. What qualities did Ben Franklin have that enabled him to become an outstanding diplomat?
2. Ben Franklin was troubled by the fact that we were not doing exactly what we said we would do by signing the preliminary treaty. Would you agree more with him or with John Jay on this topic?
3. As an advisor to King George III in 1783, how might you try to convince him that approving this treaty was the only thing he could do?

CHALLENGES:

1. Which of the three mentioned American diplomats would later become president?
2. What advantages did Franklin have as a diplomat over the others?
3. Who was Foreign Minister of France at the time?
4. Why did Franklin wear a coonskin cap?
5. For which war ending in 1763, did France want revenge?
6. When did the English first begin to talk with the Americans about a deal? What was their first offer?
7. Which section of the United States would gain most from the right to fish off the Great Bank?
8. Why didn't Jay want to make a joint U.S.-French deal with the English?
9. Who were the Loyalists? What was promised to them?
10. What would be the western boundary of the new nation?

NATIONAL STANDARDS CORRELATIONS:

NCSS IIc: (Time, Continuity, & Change) Identify and describe selected historical periods and patterns of change within and across cultures, such as the rise of civilizations, the development of transportation systems, the growth and breakdown of colonial systems, and others.
NSH Era 3, Standard 1: The causes of the American Revolution, the ideas and interests involved in forging the revolutionary movement, and the reasons for the American victory

WEBSITES:

http://www.yale.edu/lawweb/avalon/diplomacy/britain/paris.htm
"The Paris Peace Treaty of September 3, 1783," The Avalon Project at Yale Law School

http://memory.loc.gov/learn/features/timeline/amrev/peace/peace.html
"Revolutionary War: Groping Toward Peace, 1781–1783," The Library of Congress

http://earlyamerica.com/earlyamerica/maps/peace/
"The United States at the Time of the Treaty of 1783," Archiving Early America

The States Form a Confederation

John Dickinson

The Declaration of Independence was the beginning of a new era in America. The states were quick to throw off their status as colonies and began writing their constitutions. Remembering royal controls and appointed governors, they relied now on their legislatures to rule. However, there was also a war to fight, so the role of the Second Continental Congress was continued. The states made it very clear that they were in charge and had no intention of giving up any more power than necessary.

Congress had been like a committee called to meet one problem, but it continued to meet because new problems kept coming. If they were to be permanent, however, their purpose needed to be better defined. John Dickinson of Delaware chaired the committee that drafted the Articles of Confederation, which were approved by Congress in November 1777. Careful to avoid any hint they were going to take power from the states, the new union was called a "league of friendship." Before the Articles could go into effect, all thirteen new states had to approve, and that was not easily done.

Small coastal states like Maryland fretted because other states had large land claims west of the mountains. Only if these states gave up their claims to western lands to Congress would they approve the Articles. In 1781, after western lands were turned over to Congress, Maryland gave approval.

The Articles gave Congress the power to declare war and peace, manage foreign affairs, maintain an army and navy, issue and borrow money, and control the Native Americans. Each state, no matter how large or small, got one vote. Members of Congress were chosen by the state legislature for one-year terms. Nine votes were required before any policy could be adopted, and thirteen votes were required before the Articles could be amended.

Many qualities necessary for a strong government were missing: (1) There was no president or executive at the head. (2) It had no power to tax; money was raised by begging it from the states and by borrowing. (3) State support was needed but not received. States, when asked for money, often declined. Sometimes states failed to appoint delegates, and many times, there was no quorum in Congress. (4) Members of Congress often did not take their responsibility seriously, and the public ignored them. (5) Congress had no power to enforce the peace treaty after it was signed. States did not return Loyalist property, and when English merchants tried to collect from American debtors, state judges found many reasons to rule in the debtors' favor. (6) The lack of unified control in America made the threat of foreign involvement more likely. (7) Congress's inability to pay the army's back wages made the threat of a military takeover a possibility.

RESULTS: The Articles provided a temporary means for the states to work together through the Revolution, but a better approach was needed for the nation to survive. Two major pieces of legislation came out of the Confederation period. The Land Ordinance of 1785 provided a means for surveying western lands and dividing them into townships. The Northwest Ordinance of 1787 provided a system for governing the Old Northwest and creating new states.

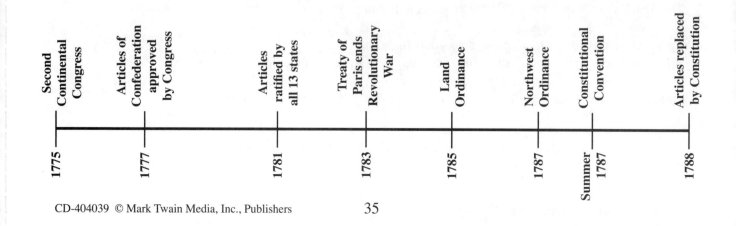

Timeline:
- 1775 — Second Continental Congress
- 1777 — Articles of Confederation approved by Congress
- 1781 — Articles ratified by all 13 states
- 1783 — Treaty of Paris ends Revolutionary War
- 1785 — Land Ordinance
- 1787 — Northwest Ordinance
- Summer 1787 — Constitutional Convention
- 1788 — Articles replaced by Constitution

Name: _____ Date: _____

The States Form a Confederation: Reinforcement

Directions: Complete the following activities, essays, and challenges on your own paper.

ACTIVITIES:

1. Discuss what would have happened if the Articles had not been approved.
2. Discuss how the Articles could be seen as a necessary step on the road toward the Constitution.

ESSAYS:

1. Why is the power to tax so important to a government? Present arguments that might have been given in 1777 for giving the Confederation the power to tax.
2. As a member of Congress who was present today when only three other members showed up, write a letter home to your family expressing your feelings about the job.
3. Some people worried that they had created a monster that endangered the freedom of the people. Do you think the Confederation was in any way a menace to liberty? Why?

CHALLENGES:

1. If Congress had no money, and delegates to Congress were chosen by the states, who paid their salaries?
2. List three powers Congress had, and tell why each was important.
3. List three things Congress could not do during the Confederation, and tell why each was important.
4. Who was chairman of the committee that wrote the Articles?
5. What allowed the Northwest to be divided into townships?
6. How many more votes did Virginia have than Rhode Island in the Confederation Congress?

NATIONAL STANDARDS CORRELATIONS:

NCSS VIb: (Power, Authority, & Governance) Describe the purpose of government and how its powers are acquired, used, and justified.
NSH Era 3, Standard 2: The impact of the American Revolution on politics, economy, and society

WEBSITES:

http://www.yale.edu/lawweb/avalon/artconf.htm
"Articles of Confederation," The Avalon Project at Yale Law School

http://bensguide.gpo.gov/6-8/documents/articles/
"The Articles of Confederation," U.S. Government Printing Office

http://www.cr.nps.gov/history/online_books/dube/inde3.htm
"A Multitude of Amendments, Alterations and Additions: Articles of Confederation," National Park Service

Old Soldiers Threaten Civilian Rule

Throughout the war, George Washington had more than just the English to contend with; he also had jealous officers who felt *they* should be in command, not him. Brigadier General Thomas Conway organized a plot against Washington during the war, but it backfired, and Conway was forced out of the army. More serious was the threat of General Horatio Gates, who made no secret of his feeling that he was the better general and should be leading the army.

General Horatio Gates

When the war ended, the soldiers returned to their shops and farms, but Congress had no money to pay their back wages. Their only currency, the "continentals," had been put out with great speed but without anything to back it. Those who had served their country were mostly poor men with families to support. In those days, there were debtors' prisons for people who did not pay their bills. As creditors pressured them to pay their debts, the old soldiers became restless.

In 1782, Colonel Lewis Nicola wrote an urgent letter to Washington suggesting that he take over as king; Washington replied that no idea caused him so much pain as to realize that such ideas were even thought of by his army. But anger with Congress was not easily solved.

Washington received warnings that discontent was strong, and some in the army had strong ambitions. At the military camp at Newburgh, New York, protest letters were being passed around, and a meeting of officers was arranged. It was assumed that Washington would not attend the meeting, but they were wrong. The general came to the front, tried to reassure them, and advised them to do nothing to stir up public discontent. He had accomplished nothing; the officers sat grim and determined. Then he remembered a letter he had received from a Congressman and pulled it out of his coat. He started to read, but the letters blurred in front of him. He reached in his pocket and pulled out eyeglasses. Few had ever seen him with glasses. He apologized, "Gentlemen, you will permit me to put on my spectacles, for I have not only grown gray, but almost blind in the service of my country." Many of the soldiers wept, and the meeting ended with the passing of a resolution expressing confidence in Congress.

Problems were far from over, as revolts by some state militias indicated. In Rhode Island, debtor farmers got control of the legislature and began to put out worthless paper money to pay off debts. The New Hampshire legislature was surrounded by mobs demanding cheap paper money; the militia came to their rescue.

The most serious trouble came in Massachusetts, where former Captain Daniel Shays led a group of discontented poor farmers. They were angry when courts tried to seize their property because they couldn't pay their taxes. The revolt was finally put down, but it was a warning of more trouble ahead unless a stronger government could be formed.

RESULTS: The Confederation was not capable of paying its soldiers or its debts. The threat that old soldiers might take over was real. Unless an answer came soon, the goal of freedom would be lost, not to a foreign king, but to leaders who might exploit the desperation of old soldiers.

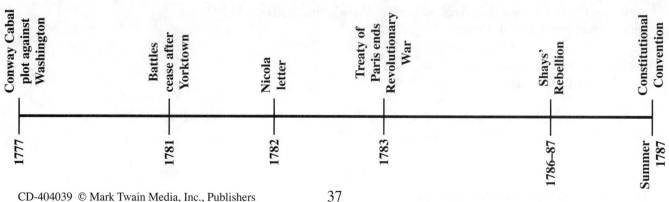

Conway Cabal plot against Washington	Battles cease after Yorktown	Nicola letter	Treaty of Paris ends Revolutionary War	Shays' Rebellion	Constitutional Convention
1777	1781	1782	1783	1786–87	Summer 1787

Name: _____ Date: _____

Old Soldiers Threaten Civilian Rule: Reinforcement

Directions: Complete the following activities, essays, and challenges on your own paper.

ACTIVITIES:

1. Discuss the attitudes you might have heard expressed at Newburgh. Why was that gathering dangerous to Congress and state governments?
2. Discuss how Shays' Rebellion looked to reformers, conservatives, debtors, and creditors.

ESSAYS:

1. An offer was made to Washington that he become king. Suppose he had decided to take the offer. What effect would that have had on history?
2. As a discharged soldier, how would you feel about the way you had been treated by Congress? Write a letter to your governor.
3. Times were hard after the Revolutionary War. How do hard times sometimes lead to violent actions on the streets?

CHALLENGES:

1. What was the term for the money a soldier in the army received?
2. Why was General Gates more of a threat than Thomas Conway had been?
3. What did Colonel Nicola suggest that made Washington so angry?
4. What was the complaint of soldiers who had left the army?
5. Which legislature was putting out worthless paper money?
6. Which legislature was threatened by mobs? How were they saved?
7. In which state did Daniel Shays live?
8. What gesture by Washington changed the minds of soldiers at Newburgh?
9. What was the chief complaint of those involved in Shays' Rebellion?
10. Why were militia a threat to state governments and Congress?

NATIONAL STANDARDS CORRELATIONS:

NCSS Xf: (Civic Ideals & Practices) Identify and explain the roles of formal and informal political actors in influencing and shaping public policy and decision-making.
NSH Era 3, Standard 2: The impact of the American Revolution on politics, economy, and society

WEBSITES:

http://www.digitalhistory.uh.edu/database/article_display.cfm?HHID=281
"Shays' Rebellion," Digital History

http://www.ushistory.org/march/other/cabal.htm
"The Conway Cabal," Independence Hall Association

http://memory.loc.gov/cgi-bin/query/r?ammem/mgw:@field(DOCID+@lit(gw240295))
"George Washington to Lewis Nicola, May 22, 1782," The Library of Congress

The Calling of the Constitutional Convention

James Madison

After retiring from the army, Washington wanted to spend the rest of his life in peace at home at Mt. Vernon, but he kept getting disturbing information that could not be ignored. British forts were still standing on American soil; the French were demanding that the bankrupt Congress repay their loans, and Spanish agents were working among the Native Americans. The continental currency was a joke, and states were taxing imports from foreign countries and other states. This was leading to fierce arguments between states. Congress had little power under the Articles. Shays' Rebellion had demonstrated growing public disorder. Fear of a military takeover was always present. Unless something was done soon, everything Washington had fought for would be lost.

A new approach to solving the nation's problems began to appear. In 1785, Virginia and Maryland delegates met at Mt. Vernon to work out problems of trade on the Potomac River. The meeting went very well, so it was decided that another conference should take place the following year at Annapolis, with all thirteen states invited. Only five states sent delegates to Annapolis, but Alexander Hamilton suggested that another meeting be held in Philadelphia in 1787, to consider changing defects in the Articles of Confederation. Congress gave a feeble endorsement to the proposal, and states were asked to choose delegates to go to the meeting.

At the time, Washington suffered from malaria and rheumatism, but when asked to go, he accepted. That news gave special meaning to the gathering, and states began to choose talented men for their delegations. The average delegate was in his early forties, although Ben Franklin, who was now 80 years old, raised that average. Most were college educated, had served in state legislatures or Congress, and were financially well off. Lawyers, merchants, and farmers were overly represented; no poor men, women, or minorities participated.

To no one's surprise, Washington was chosen president of the convention. The delegates made an important early decision to keep the proceedings secret; compromising was easier if no one was giving headlines to the press. A few delegates, including James Madison, took notes on the debates. Later, these would be important to historians since the official minutes gave only a brief outline of what was said and decided.

Much compromising went on as delegates from large and small states, North and South, commercial and agricultural states, liberals and conservatives, struggled to find the words upon which they could agree. Fortunately, they all believed there should be *three branches of government* (legislative, executive, and judicial), and each should be independent of interference from the others. They believed in *checks and balances*, so each could stop the others from grabbing power. All believed in *republican government,* one where supreme power rests with the people.

RESULTS: Out of this meeting came the Constitution of the United States, an incredible document that has served the nation for over 200 years and has only been amended 27 times.

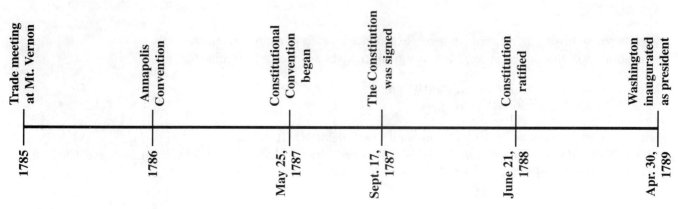

Trade meeting at Mt. Vernon	Annapolis Convention	Constitutional Convention began	The Constitution was signed	Constitution ratified	Washington inaugurated as president
1785	1786	May 25, 1787	Sept. 17, 1787	June 21, 1788	Apr. 30, 1789

Name: _____ Date: _____

The Calling of the Constitutional Convention: Reinforcement

Directions: Complete the following activities, essays, and challenges on your own paper.

ACTIVITIES:

1. Have students look at the organization of the Constitution and see how it is in a logical order.
2. The Constitution does not trust anyone with unlimited power. Have students look in Article I, Section 8, to see limits on the power of the president as commander in chief.

ESSAYS:

1. The Convention closed its doors, and all the delegates agreed to keep their discussions secret. If you had been present, what arguments would you have given for or against that idea?
2. The Constitution gave members of the House two-year terms, senators were given six-year terms, and the president was given a four-year term. Do you think there should be limits on the number of terms a person can serve? Why?
3. No one was completely happy with everything in the Constitution. What might have happened if all the members had gotten angry and left?

CHALLENGES:

1. Who suggested that a meeting be held in Philadelphia? What was said to be the reason for the meeting?
2. What countries were causing the Confederation trouble in 1787?
3. At whose home did the Mt. Vernon Conference take place?
4. Who was the oldest delegate at the Constitutional Convention?
5. Who took notes at the meeting? Why were those notes important later?
6. Which term used in the article is closest to another term, "representative government"?
7. What is meant by "checks and balances"?
8. Why didn't Washington want to go?
9. What are the three branches of government? What government officials are at the top of each?
10. The Bill of Rights is the first ten Amendments and was added in 1791. After that, how many times has the Constitution been amended?

NATIONAL STANDARDS CORRELATIONS:

NCSS VIb: (Power, Authority, & Governance) Describe the purpose of government and how its powers are acquired, used, and justified.

NSH Era 3, Standard 3: The institutions and practices of government created during the Revolution and how they were revised between 1787 and 1815 to create the foundation of the American political system based on the U.S. Constitution and the Bill of Rights.

WEBSITES:

http://www.archives.gov/national_archives_experience/charters/constitution.html#more
"Constitution of the United States," U.S. National Archives and Records Administration

http://www.loc.gov/exhibits/treasures/trt049.html
"The Federalist," The Library of Congress

http://memory.loc.gov/cgi-bin/query/r?ammem/hlaw:@field(DOCID+@lit(fr003134)%20)
"The Records of the Federal Convention of 1787 [Farrand's Records, Volume 3] CXIX. William Pierce: Character Sketches of Delegates to the Federal Convention," The Library of Congress

Washington Stays Calm in Stormy Times

Edmond Genet

Despite his reputation as a general, George Washington much preferred a farm field to a battlefield or an inspection of his mules to a review of his troops. He could never be just a peaceful farmer again. When duty called, he answered. When the Constitutional Convention created the office of president, everyone there knew who would be chosen. The Electoral College unanimously chose him, and once again, Washington left his farm to serve his nation. He did not want the job and wrote that his feelings were like those of the criminal on the way to be executed.

He organized his administration around old and trusted friends: Alexander Hamilton was secretary of the treasury, Henry Knox was secretary of war, and Thomas Jefferson was secretary of state. In domestic affairs, the government would bring order to the chaos of the Confederation period. Hamilton's policies not only paid the government's bills, but paid the Confederation's and the state war debts. Federal taxes were levied and collected. When Western farmers rioted against the tax on whiskey, Washington sent militia units into the riot area, and order was restored. The ringleaders of the rebellion were arrested, but Washington pardoned them. He did not want to fill prisons; he just wanted Americans to obey the law.

Most of Washington's concerns were in foreign affairs. In July 1789, a few months after Washington took the oath of office, the French Revolution broke out, and Americans were thrilled that the French had followed their example. French mobs began to cut off the heads of noblemen, and in January 1793, they executed King Louis XVI and his wife. In February, France declared war on England. Federalists supported England, but Republicans favored the French. Washington knew that getting involved in this affair would be dangerous for the United States, so he issued a Proclamation of Neutrality. He warned that Americans helping either side would be punished. The new French minister (ambassador) arrived soon afterward. His name was Edmond Genet. He ignored Washington's policy by persuading Americans to raid English ships. After repeated warnings, Washington decided to expel Genet from the United States. Genet then reversed himself and begged for permission to stay.

The English captured American ships and forced American sailors to either join the British navy or they were sent to prisons with terrible conditions. Frontiersmen feared Native-American attacks as long as British forts existed on American soil. Washington asked Chief Justice John Jay to go to England and work out a treaty. The Jay Treaty (1795) only did part of what needed to be done. The English did promise to leave the forts, but other problems were left to be taken care of later. The treaty barely got the two-thirds approval of the Senate that the Constitution required. It passed, 20–10.

RESULTS: After eight years as president, Washington retired. Before he left office, he gave parting advice to the nation in his farewell address. He warned against forming political parties because they divided the people when national unity was required. He also warned against permanent alliances with other nations that might draw America into their wars.

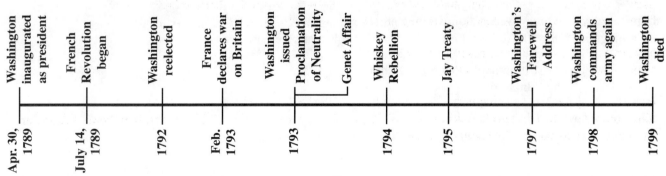

Washington inaugurated as president — Apr. 30, 1789

French Revolution began — July 14, 1789

Washington reelected — 1792

France declares war on Britain — Feb. 1793

Washington issued Proclamation of Neutrality — 1793

Genet Affair

Whiskey Rebellion — 1794

Jay Treaty — 1795

Washington's Farewell Address — 1797

Washington commands army again — 1798

Washington died — 1799

Name: _____ Date: _____

Washington Stays Calm in Stormy Times: Reinforcement

Directions: Complete the following activities, essays, and challenges on your own paper.

ACTIVITIES:

1. Discuss the role of the Cabinet. (You might point out that the president's Cabinet size has grown because the needs have changed in our society today.)
2. Have students discuss why we should or should not have helped the French after they helped us.

ESSAYS:

1. Washington thought political parties caused harmful divisions among the American people. Do you agree? Why or why not?
2. Discuss the way in which Washington handled the Whiskey Rebellion. Do you think he was right or wrong in not punishing the leaders?
3. Washington was the only president chosen by unanimous vote of the Electoral College. Why is that a record very unlikely to be broken?

CHALLENGES:

1. Who was Washington's secretary of state? What role does a secretary of state have in government?
2. Which group of Americans supported France in its war with England?
3. How did Washington keep the Whiskey Rebellion under control?
4. Whose powers are discussed in Article II of the Constitution?
5. Who was Edmond Genet, and how did he anger Washington?
6. Why did Washington think the United States should stay out of the war between England and France?
7. How excited was Washington about being chosen as president?
8. What was the main accomplishment of the Jay Treaty?
9. How did Washington feel about political parties?
10. What is an alliance? Why did Washington warn against permanent alliances?

NATIONAL STANDARDS CORRELATIONS:

<u>NCSS Xf:</u> (Civic Ideals & Practices) Identify and explain the roles of formal and informal political actors in influencing and shaping public policy and decision-making.

<u>NSH Era 3, Standard 3:</u> The institutions and practices of government created during the Revolution and how they were revised between 1787 and 1815 to create the foundation of the American political system based on the U.S. Constitution and the Bill of Rights

WEBSITES:

http://www.yale.edu/lawweb/avalon/presiden/inaug/wash1.htm
"First Inaugural Address of George Washington," The Avalon Project at Yale Law School

http://www.yale.edu/lawweb/avalon/washing.htm
"Washington's Farewell Address 1796," The Avalon Project at Yale Law School

http://www.loc.gov/rr/program/bib/ourdocs/jay.html
"Jay's Treaty," The Library of Congress

http://www.nps.gov/frhi/whiskreb.htm
"The Whiskey Rebellion," National Park Service

Eli Whitney Invents the Cotton Gin

Eli Whitney

Slavery was an unpopular institution by the 1790s. Northern states abolished slavery by court action or by laws they passed. Southerners had too much money invested in slaves to go that far, but they did make it easier for owners to free their slaves if they wished. The main use for slaves was tobacco production, but the crop was hard on the soil. Washington and many other people felt slavery would end someday because it was not profitable.

There were two varieties of cotton: upland and sea island. Of the two, sea island had the longest fibers and was the easiest to clean (to remove the seeds). Upland cotton would grow best in the South, but those pesky seeds were hard to untangle from the cotton boll.

Eli Whitney was from New England; as a boy he liked to invent and repair things. He worked his way through Yale by fixing the college's equipment. A carpenter said to him, "There was one good mechanic spoiled when you went to college." He wanted to study law, but that required money he did not have, so he became a tutor on a Georgia plantation. There he overheard farmers discussing their problems. If only someone could devise a way to remove the seeds from cotton, the Southern farmer could become more productive. Whitney began work on a machine.

The timing was perfect because another man, whom Whitney did not know, was going to make his machine especially useful. The man was Samuel Slater, who had escaped from England with plans for a cotton mill sketched in his mind. Landing in Rhode Island, he and some other men built the first cotton mill in America. The combination of a product, the means to develop it, and a world market desiring it, is a sure road to success.

Whitney's machine was called a "cotton gin." It was a box with a hand-cranked cylinder that fed the cotton through narrow slots wide enough for the cotton but too narrow for the seeds. The seeds dropped to the bottom and out of the way. When improvements were made to it, one person could do in a day what had taken months to do before. Whitney and his partner, Phineas Miller, patented their machine, but imitators quickly made copies of it. Whitney never made much money from that machine; however, he did get a government contract to produce muskets. To save costs, he used molds to make the same parts for each gun. It was the beginning of interchangeable parts, a system that makes mass production possible today.

RESULTS: In 1792, the United States produced 10,000 bales of cotton. By 1825, the year Whitney died, the cotton states produced 533,000 bales. Cotton products were far more popular than wool for clothing; and with the means to produce cotton cloth expanding, it was more affordable.

There were also negative consequences. Expansion of cotton production required more workers, and that made a new market for slaves. The price of slaves shot up, and the South would never voluntarily surrender this large pool of workers. Efforts to purchase slaves and return them to Africa (colonizing) were of little effect because of the rising price of slaves.

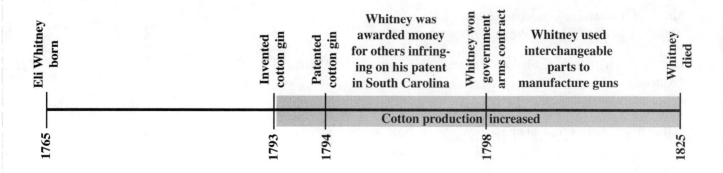

| Eli Whitney born | Invented cotton gin | Patented cotton gin | Whitney was awarded money for others infring-ing on his patent in South Carolina | Whitney won government arms contract | Whitney used interchangeable parts to manufacture guns | Whitney died |

Cotton production increased

1765   1793   1794   1798   1825

Name: _____ Date: _____

Eli Whitney Invents the Cotton Gin: Reinforcement

Directions: Complete the following activities, essays, and challenges on your own paper.

ACTIVITIES:

1. Discuss the sacrifices an inventor makes, and ask whether it is worth the cost.
2. Discuss how an invention sometimes has unfortunate side effects. (You might use atomic energy as an example.)

ESSAYS:

1. Whitney's cotton gin actually made very little money for him because of others who used his concept to design their own. Does this present a problem today for inventors and musicians? Give examples.
2. The article mentioned the importance of a product, a means to produce the product, and a need for it. Give some examples to show how that applies to a modern device.

CHALLENGES:

1. For every bale of cotton produced in 1792, how many were produced in 1825?
2. Why did people think slavery was dying in 1790?
3. What is meant by cleaning cotton?
4. What did the carpenter mean by his remark, "There was one good mechanic spoiled when you went to college"?
5. What advantages did sea island cotton have over upland cotton?
6. What kind of cotton grew best in the American South?
7. What was cotton's chief competitor as a Southern cash crop?
8. How did the cotton gin affect the price of clothing? Why?
9. What other process was changed by Whitney? Why was it important?
10. What was the worst side effect of Whitney's cotton gin?

NATIONAL STANDARDS CORRELATIONS:

NCSS VIIIc: (Science, Technology, & Society) Describe examples in which values, beliefs, and attitudes have been influenced by new scientific and technological knowledge, such as the invention of the printing press, conceptions of the universe, applications of atomic energy, and genetic discoveries.
NSH Era 4, Standard 2: How the industrial revolution, increasing immigration, the rapid expansion of slavery, and the westward movement changed the lives of Americans and led toward regional tensions

WEBSITES:

http://www.eliwhitney.org/cotton.htm
"The Cotton Gin," The Eli Whitney Museum

http://www.digitalhistory.uh.edu/database/article_display.cfm?HHID=73
"Antebellum Slavery," Digital History

http://www.pbs.org/wgbh/aia/part3/3narr6.html
"Growth and Entrenchment of Slavery," Public Broadcasting Service

Matthew Lyon Defies the Sedition Act

John Adams

Matthew Lyon was an angry man in 1798, but that was nothing new to him. As a Republican in Federalist Vermont, he was often in the minority, and in those days, tempers ran hot when it came to politics. As a member of the House, he got into a heated argument with Representative Robert Griswold of Connecticut, and the two men tumbled to the floor in a brawl, wielding a cane and firetongs. His low opinion of John Adams was well known; he had expressed it often enough in his newspaper. When the Sedition Act was passed, he would either have to be quiet or face time in prison.

The Sedition Act had been passed as a response to recent actions by the French. Angry over the Jay Treaty, which the Federalists had passed, the French stubbornly refused to approve the minister (ambassador) sent by the incoming president, John Adams. Rather than give in to the demands of some hot-headed Federalists for war, Adams sent three men to France to try and work things out. They were visited one night by three representatives of Foreign Minister Talleyrand. If the Americans gave Talleyrand a bribe, they would be allowed to talk with him. The Americans refused to pay the bribe and returned home. Adams sent a report of this insult to Congress and referred to the French agents as X, Y, and Z, and so the incident was called the XYZ Affair.

Federalists saw this as an opportunity for political advantage over the pro-French Republicans. With patriotism running high, they increased the size of the army and navy and began to capture armed French merchant ships at sea. They then went even further and passed the Alien and Sedition Acts. The Alien Act extended the time before a person could become a citizen from five years to fourteen years. The reason behind this was that immigrants were all joining the Republican party. The law also gave the president power to deport undesirable aliens.

The Sedition Act made it a crime to spread "false, scandalous, and malicious" writing against the government, the president, or Congress that would bring any of them into contempt or disrepute. Under this law, fifteen people were charged and ten found guilty. One of these was Matthew Lyon, who criticized "aristocratic hirelings from the English porcupine." The judge, who was an ardent Federalist, sentenced Lyon to four months in jail and a $1,000 fine. He was taken to a jail usually used for common criminals. Friends wanted to rescue him, but he told them to vote their opinion, and he was reelected by a very large margin. After friends paid the fine, he was released and then returned to Philadelphia accompanied by a long line of supporters. Rather than silencing criticism, the Sedition Act had only made the Federalists look like enemies of freedom.

RESULTS: A number of other critics were heard as well. The Virginia and Kentucky legislatures passed resolutions protesting the law. The secret authors of those resolutions were James Madison and Thomas Jefferson. The Alien Act was repealed, and the Sedition Act expired. The French saw that their policy had been a big mistake, and they accepted new American diplomats with proper dignity, without asking for a bribe. However, Lyon continued to speak his mind.

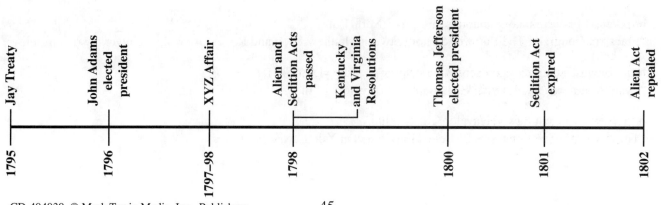

Name: _____ Date: _____

Matthew Lyon Defies the Sedition Act: Reinforcement

Directions: Complete the following activities, essays, and challenges on your own paper.

ACTIVITIES:

1. Discuss student opinions of the Sedition Act and how Congress and the public sometimes overreact to a tense situation.
2. Discuss whether or not students think Lyon was a great man for the way he stood up to Adams.

ESSAYS:

1. The Supreme Court had not yet claimed the power to declare an act of Congress unconstitutional. If it had, what do you think it would have said about the Sedition Act? (Look up the First Amendment.)
2. How do you think citizens should react to a law they consider harmful to their liberties?
3. Politics were very rough in the 1790s, and politicians said very mean and unfair things about opponents. Do you think there should be limits on what is said by politicians? Why or why not?

CHALLENGES:

1. What were the terms of the Alien Act?
2. Why was the Alien Act passed?
3. What position in government did Matthew Lyon hold?
4. How did Lyon feel about President Adams?
5. Who were X, Y, and Z?
6. How did Americans respond to the XYZ Affair?
7. What happened when Lyon was brought to trial?
8. Who secretly wrote the Kentucky and Virginia resolutions?
9. Research Thomas Jefferson. What position did he hold in government at the time of the Sedition Act?
10. What finally happened to the Alien and Sedition Acts?

NATIONAL STANDARDS CORRELATIONS:

NCSS VI: (Power, Authority, & Governance) Examine persistent issues involving the rights, roles, and status of the individual in relation to the general welfare.
NSH Era 3, Standard 3: The institutions and practices of government created during the Revolution and how they were revised between 1787 and 1815 to create the foundation of the American political system based on the U.S. Constitution and the Bill of Rights

WEBSITES:

http://etext.lib.virginia.edu/journals/EH/EH41/Neff41.html
"Fracas in Congress: The Battle of Honor between Matthew Lyon and Roger Griswold," University of Virginia

http://bioguide.congress.gov/scripts/biodisplay.pl?index=L000545
"Lyon, Matthew, (1749–1822)," Biographical Directory of the United States Congress

http://www.yale.edu/lawweb/avalon/alsedact.htm
"The Alien and Seditions Acts," The Avalon Project at Yale Law School

Opportunity Knocks: Jefferson Responds

Thomas Jefferson

Never had an opportunity like this come to the United States; Jefferson knew it, but he was still troubled by it. Here was a chance to buy 827,000 square miles of real estate, rid the nation of a dangerous neighbor, and allow room for expansion to the crest of the Rocky Mountains. It had come about in this way: France had lost its domain known as Louisiana to Spain in 1763, but French pride had been hurt in the process. In 1800, Napoleon had put pressure on Spain to return it, and the two nations had made a secret treaty whereby France could take it back whenever they chose. American diplomats heard rumors of this deal in 1801.

People didn't know much about Louisiana at the time. There were only a few settlements like St. Louis on its eastern fringe, but what it held in rivers, minerals, animals, and agricultural potential was anyone's guess. It was known there were many Native Americans there, but their numbers and friendship were yet to be discovered. What was known was, in the hands of Spain, Louisiana was no threat to western development. If France moved back in, it could block American expansion and, at worst, become a hazard to the United States. Jefferson told American diplomats to use whatever means they could to prevent the transfer of the land from Spain to France.

That need was emphasized when the Spanish governor at New Orleans issued an order that would prevent Americans from depositing their goods at New Orleans while waiting for ships to transport them to world markets. Frontiersmen suspected the French were behind this and were willing to take steps to seize New Orleans. To calm them down, Jefferson sent James Monroe to Paris with instructions to buy New Orleans and Florida if France owned them. Before Monroe arrived, Napoleon had already decided to sell the Louisiana Territory. He had hoped to use it to feed the people of Haiti while they produced sugar and tropical fruit for France, but his plan had fallen through. Led by Toussaint L'Ouverture, the Haitians had destroyed a French army sent to control them. Without Haiti, Napoleon did not need Louisiana.

The price agreed upon for the Louisiana Territory was $15,000,000, one-fourth of which was to pay damage claims by Americans against the French; however, the deal bothered the president's conscience. No specific authority had been given by the Constitution to buy land, and he had always opposed stretching the language of the Constitution. He thought about seeking a Constitutional amendment, but Monroe advised him that Napoleon would back out if they delayed. The temptation was too strong, and Jefferson took the offer to Congress. It approved the treaty and the money. The Louisiana Territory now belonged to the United States.

The Louisiana Purchase also removed Republican reluctance to use the elastic clause of the Constitution whenever it was convenient.

RESULTS: It would take many years before the full potential of the Louisiana Territory would be known. Lewis and Clark's expedition was a helpful beginning in discovering the Upper Missouri River region, and Zebulon Pike was sent to find the source of the Arkansas River. Other secrets of the region would be discovered by fur trappers and pioneers.

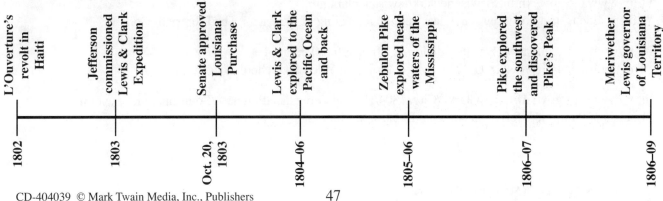

L'Ouverture's revolt in Haiti	Jefferson commissioned Lewis & Clark Expedition	Senate approved Louisiana Purchase	Lewis & Clark explored to the Pacific Ocean and back	Zebulon Pike explored headwaters of the Mississippi	Pike explored the southwest and discovered Pike's Peak	Meriwether Lewis governor of Louisiana Territory
1802	1803	Oct. 20, 1803	1804–06	1805–06	1806–07	1806–09

Name: _____ Date: _____

Opportunity Knocks: Jefferson Responds: Reinforcement

Directions: Complete the following activities, essays, and challenges on your own paper.

ACTIVITIES:

1. Look at a map, and identify the states that grew out of the Louisiana Purchase.
2. Have students research the Lewis and Clark Expedition.

ESSAYS:

1. Jefferson went against his conscience in approving the Louisiana Purchase. Was this a good idea? Discuss the pros and cons of a modern president doing the same thing to achieve his goal.
2. Why would the Louisiana Purchase be important to America's national development?
3. As a strict constructionist from the West, what would you think about the Louisiana Purchase?

CHALLENGES:

1. Who ruled France in 1803?
2. Why were Americans not upset about the treaty between France and Spain until a year after it was signed?
3. Why were Westerners worried in 1802?
4. How much money did France actually receive for Louisiana?
5. What legal problem with the deal worried Jefferson?
6. Why did he go ahead with the deal despite his concerns?
7. Whom did Jefferson send to France to help Robert Livingston, the U.S. minister to France, make the deal?
8. How did Toussaint L'Ouverture help the United States?
9. What explorers went to the Upper Missouri River region?
10. A strict constructionist believed the United States could only do what the Constitution specifically allowed. A loose constructionist believed the U.S. could do whatever was "necessary and proper" to carry out its responsibilities listed in Article I, Section 8, of the Constitution. Was Jefferson's purchase of Louisiana an example of strict construction or loose construction? Why?

NATIONAL STANDARDS CORRELATIONS:

NCSS VIc: (Power, Authority, & Governance) Analyze and explain ideas and governmental mechanisms to meet needs and wants of citizens, regulate territory, manage conflict, and establish order and security.
NSH Era 4, Standard 1: United States territorial expansion between 1801 and 1861, and how it affected relations with external powers and Native Americans

WEBSITES:

http://www.loc.gov/exhibits/lewisandclark/lewisandclark.html
"Rivers, Edens, Empires: Lewis & Clark and the Revealing of America," The Library of Congress

http://www.yale.edu/lawweb/avalon/diplomacy/france/fr1803m.html
"The Louisiana Purchase: 1803," The Avalon Project at Yale Law School

http://www.nps.gov/jeff/LewisClark2/Circa1804/Heritage/LouisianaPurchase/LouisianaPurchase.htm
"Louisiana Purchase," Jefferson National Expansion Memorial

John Marshall Declares an Act of Congress Unconstitutional

John Marshall

Although he probably didn't realize it, President Adams made his longest-lasting decision in the selection of John Marshall to the Supreme Court. It wasn't easy finding high-quality men for the Court in those days. The job required long horseback rides, staying in dingy inns, and listening to endless debates between lawyers. The Court only met briefly each year in the capital because so few cases were appealed. The workload was so light that Chief Justice Jay took time to negotiate a treaty in England. His successor, Oliver Ellsworth, was also sent on a diplomatic mission to France.

Marshall had been a captain during the Revolution and then became a lawyer. He was a delegate to Virginia's convention ratifying the Constitution and served a term in the U.S. House. He was a quiet, friendly man. He did not appear impressive, but in debate or a courtroom, he moved quickly to the heart of issues. As a strong Federalist, he had won the admiration of Washington and Adams. Since he was only 46 years old, he could take the punishment of the travels required by the job.

The Supreme Court consisted of six justices at that time. The issues they could decide were set in Article III of the Constitution, and can be summarized as: (1) Appellate power in cases involving federal law and treaties and (2) direct power in disputes between states and cases involving ambassadors. When not meeting as a court, the justices rode circuit. The Judiciary Act of 1789, said that a Court of Appeals would consist of two Supreme Court justices and a district judge. That was the reason many qualified men were not interested in the court.

Other people were also appointed by Adams, including some appointees in 1801. Because they were appointed at the last minute, they were called the "midnight judges." One of those was William Marbury, appointed to be a justice of the peace in the District of Columbia. After confirmation by the Senate, their papers were signed by the president and then taken to the office of the secretary of state. Once the Great Seal of the United States was on these documents, the new officers could perform their jobs.

Jefferson's choice for secretary of state was James Madison. When he saw the documents on his desk, he asked Jefferson what to do with them. Jefferson realized that he could keep sixteen Federalists from holding office simply by withholding these commissions, and he told Madison to hold them. Marbury used a clause in the Judiciary Act to sue in the Supreme Court for his commission. The case is known as *Marbury v. Madison* and is one of the most important decisions ever made by the Court. Under the Judiciary Act, Marbury was entitled to his commission. However, the Constitution had not given the Supreme Court authority to hear this type of case as original jurisdiction. No government official could go beyond the powers given by the Constitution, including the Supreme Court, so the Judiciary Act was declared unconstitutional.

RESULTS: For the first time, the Court established the principle of judicial review and its power to declare an act of Congress invalid.

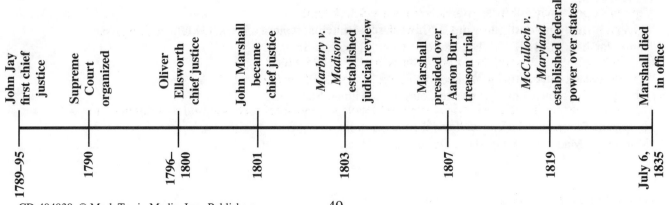

John Jay first chief justice	Supreme Court organized	Oliver Ellsworth chief justice	John Marshall became chief justice	*Marbury v. Madison* established judicial review	Marshall presided over Aaron Burr treason trial	*McCulloch v. Maryland* established federal power over states	Marshall died in office
1789–95	1790	1796–1800	1801	1803	1807	1819	July 6, 1835

Name: _____ Date: _____

John Marshall Declares an Act of Congress Unconstitutional: Reinforcement

Directions: Complete the following activities, essays, and challenges on your own paper.

ACTIVITIES:

1. Research the Supreme Court and its powers today. How much does the modern court owe to John Marshall's court?
2. Research a recent Supreme Court case, and have students define words describing decisions: unanimous, majority, concurring, dissenting.

ESSAYS:

1. John Marshall served on the Supreme Court thirty-five years, longer than any other Chief Justice. Do you think it is a good idea to allow judges to serve for long periods of time? Why?
2. When the Supreme Court disagrees with Congress, which do you think should win the argument? Why?
3. Research John Marshall and list some of his other famous decisions.

CHALLENGES:

1. What office had Marshall held in the legislative branch?
2. How many men were on the Supreme Court after Ellsworth resigned and before Marshall was confirmed?
3. To what political party did Marshall belong?
4. What was there about being on the Supreme Court that made the life of a justice difficult?
5. Why was Marbury called a "midnight judge"?
6. What law was Marbury trying to use to get his papers?
7. "Original jurisdiction" means that a court is the first to hear a particular type of case. What is meant by "appellate jurisdiction"?
8. Over which types of cases does the Supreme Court have original jurisdiction?
9. Why did Jefferson not want to give these men the commissions to which they were entitled?
10. What is judicial review? Why is it important?

NATIONAL STANDARDS CORRELATIONS:

NCSS VIb: (Power, Authority, & Governance) Describe the purpose of government and how its powers are acquired, used, and justified.

NSH Era 3, Standard 3: The institutions and practices of government created during the Revolution and how they were revised between 1787 and 1815 to create the foundation of the American political system based on the U.S. Constitution and the Bill of Rights

WEBSITES:

http://www.supremecourthistory.org/02_history/subs_timeline/images_chiefs/004.html
"John Marshall: 1801–1835," The Supreme Court Historical Society

http://www.supremecourtus.gov/
"About the Supreme Court," Supreme Court of the United States

http://usinfo.state.gov/usa/infousa/facts/democrac/9.htm
"Marbury v. Madison (1803)," U.S. Department of State

"Fulton's Folly" Changes Transportation

Robert Fulton

Water transportation was little different in 1800 than it had been 1,800 years before. It was still boats powered by wind or oars, moving a little faster than the current downstream, and painfully slow upstream. On America's western rivers, a variety of canoes, rafts, and flatboats could be seen. But one American had a vision of an improved method, and while critics called it "folly," Robert Fulton proved not only that steam could drive boats, but that steamboats could bring great profit to their owners and lower prices to consumers.

Fulton was creative from his youth. When he was ten, he made his own pencils; when he was 13, he invented a skyrocket; and at 14, he devised a manually powered paddlewheel for his fishing boat. When he was 17, he began working for a silversmith. Fulton had so much nervous energy that people questioned whether he was normal. After a serious illness, he began to paint miniatures and traveled to England to visit his famous artist uncle, Benjamin West. While there, his interest turned from art to engineering.

He worked on a system of lifting boats over difficult spots in canals and invented a dredging machine for cutting canal channels. In 1797, he went to France where he studied languages, mathematics, chemistry, and physics. He offered to build a submarine for the French government. On the first test, his submarine dived 25 feet and stayed under seven minutes; the second test lasted 17 minutes. When Napoleon showed little interest in his device, he was lured to England, where there was more interest in his invention of an underwater mine called a coffer than in submarines. A mine was used against a French ship, and an angry public protested that it was an unfair weapon. After receiving payment from the English, he returned to the United States in 1806 and began working on the device that would be his crowning achievement: the steamboat.

He was not the only one trying to build a steam-powered boat. His brother-in-law, John Stevens, tried out the *Little Juliana* in 1806 but was not satisfied with the results. Fulton completed his *Clermont* the next year. His project was done so quietly that newspapers paid little attention to it, but when it chugged up the Hudson River from New York in August 1807, a fair-sized crowd came out to watch and to scoff at what was called "Fulton's Folly." To the surprise of scoffers, the *Clermont* arrived in Albany thirty-two hours later. In 1811, his *New Orleans* was the first steamboat to sail down the Ohio and Mississippi Rivers. During the War of 1812, he designed a steam warship named *Fulton the First,* but it did not see action.

RESULTS: Fulton was never popular, mainly because he kept trying to get a monopoly on steamboats, and the public opposed it. By the 1830s, many steamboats moved up and down rivers, bringing down the costs of shipping and traveling for the American public. Steamboat accidents were common, as unsafe boilers, snags in river bottoms, and sandbars took their toll. However, it was the beginning of exciting changes in transportation.

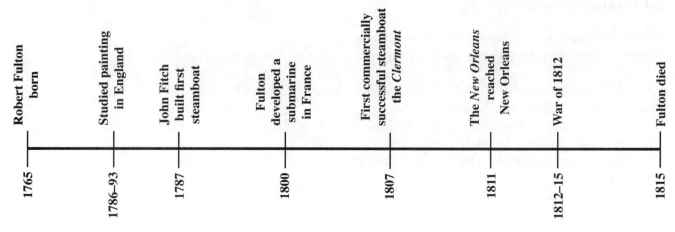

1765	1786–93	1787	1800	1807	1811	1812–15	1815
Robert Fulton born	Studied painting in England	John Fitch built first steamboat	Fulton developed a submarine in France	First commercially successful steamboat the *Clermont*	The *New Orleans* reached New Orleans	War of 1812	Fulton died

Name: _____ Date: _____

"Fulton's Folly" Changes Transportation: Reinforcement

Directions: Complete the following activities, essays, and challenges on your own paper.

ACTIVITIES:

1. Have students research early steamboats to discover whether they were sternwheelers or sidewheelers.
2. Fulton was not the first to develop a steamboat. Discuss how it is that the first does not always get success or fame.

ESSAYS:

1. What is there about inventors that makes them seem odd to other people?
2. Fulton sold his services to three nations. Do you think a modern inventor should be allowed to sell his services to other nations?
3. Fulton wanted to get rich from his steamboat, but states refused to give him complete control of their rivers. If you lived in the 1810s, would you have sided with him or the states? Why?

CHALLENGES:

1. What were some of Fulton's interests before he reached the age of 17?
2. When he traveled to England, whom did he visit?
3. What did he want to build for the French?
4. What was a "coffer"? Why do you think people thought it was unfair?
5. Who was Fulton's rival in steamboat building? How did Fulton beat him?
6. Why would a steamboat be superior to a flatboat?
7. How long did it take the *Clermont* to make the trip from New York to Albany?
8. To which three countries did Fulton provide military devices, and what did he produce for each?
9. What was the effect of steamboats on the cost of shipping goods? Why?
10. What made steamboats unsafe?

NATIONAL STANDARDS CORRELATIONS:

<u>NCSS VIIIa:</u> (Science, Technology, & Society) Examine and describe the influence of culture on scientific and technological choices and advancement, such as in transportation, medicine, and warfare.

<u>NSH Era 4, Standard 2:</u> How the industrial revolution, increasing immigration, the rapid expansion of slavery, and the westward movement changed the lives of Americans and led toward regional tensions

WEBSITES:

http://www.history.rochester.edu/steam/thurston/fulton/
"Robert Fulton: His Life and Its Treasures by Robert H. Thurston," University of Rochester

http://xroads.virginia.edu/~HYPER/DETOC/transport/fulton.html
"Robert Fulton," University of Virginia

http://memory.loc.gov/ammem/today/aug26.html
"Today in History: August 26," The Library of Congress

The United States Declares War on England in 1812

William Henry Harrison

In 1803, war broke out between England and France. This war was not the same type as before the French Revolution, because this time England's opponent was Napoleon. His method was not just to defeat an army, but to conquer the nation. At first, Americans were able to take advantage of the situation. American ships that could not carry goods between the French West Indies and France before the war were now allowed. The English considered that illegal and captured American ships. That was bad enough, Americans thought, but even worse was the impressment of sailors. The English began to stop American ships and search them for deserters from the Royal Navy. If they found a sailor who looked strong, they often took him anyway. It did no good for the sailor to complain; if he did, he would be flogged with a cat-o'-nine-tails. He would wait, and at the first opportunity, he would escape.

In 1807, the U.S. Navy ship *Chesapeake* was stopped by the *Leopard,* and the *Leopard* captain demanded that the captain of the *Chesapeake* allow his officers to search for deserters. When the American commander refused, the *Leopard* opened fire. The *Chesapeake* was not prepared for battle and after being hit many times, it surrendered. The British sailed off with four members of the crew. Americans were outraged, but because the United States had little army or navy, all Jefferson could do was order English ships to leave American ports.

That was not the only problem between the United States and England. People on the frontier worried about a Native American named Tecumseh. He saw the Native Americans selling their dignity for alcohol, then giving up their land for a few dollars. His sister had taught him that it was wrong to be cruel to an animal or a person; his brother taught him to hate whites. He mixed the two ideas. He would fight, but would not allow torture. Tecumseh's brother, the Prophet, was a medicine man claiming magical powers. Governor William Henry Harrison of Indiana Territory scoffed at those claims and said if he could do magic, then why didn't he blot out the sun? The Prophet announced the day he would blot out the sun. That day the sky grew dark, and the sun was hidden. Tecumseh had read in an almanac of a solar eclipse that day. The Native Americans were convinced and rallied around Tecumseh.

Governor Harrison formed an army and attacked the Prophet's camp at Tippecanoe. The Native Americans withdrew after the battle and left behind guns with English markings on them. To American Westerners, this was proof that the Native Americans were being armed by the British.

Henry Clay of Kentucky became the Speaker of the House in 1811, and he and his friends took a hard line toward England; for that, they were called War Hawks. The term was intended as an insult, but they liked it and used it as a badge of pride.

Angered by English restrictions on trade, impressment, and Western fears, Congress moved toward war in 1812.

RESULTS: The War of 1812 was poorly fought, but some heroes emerged—Oliver Perry and Andrew Jackson especially. The peace treaty was signed at Ghent, Belgium, in 1814, with neither side gaining land.

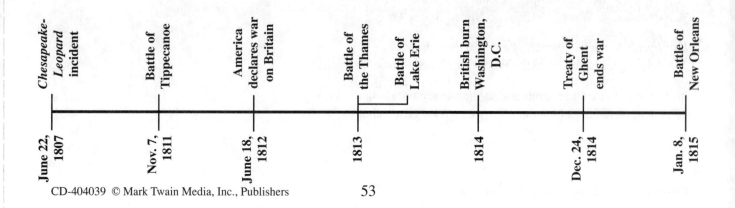

Chesapeake-Leopard incident — June 22, 1807
Battle of Tippecanoe — Nov. 7, 1811
America declares war on Britain — June 18, 1812
Battle of the Thames — 1813
Battle of Lake Erie — 1813
British burn Washington, D.C. — 1814
Treaty of Ghent ends war — Dec. 24, 1814
Battle of New Orleans — Jan. 8, 1815

Name: _____ Date: _____

The United States Declares War on
England in 1812: Reinforcement

Directions: Complete the following activities, essays, and challenges on your own paper.

ACTIVITIES:

1. The "Star-Spangled Banner" was written to describe the battle at Ft. McHenry. Have students look at the words to see Key's description of the battle and the importance to him of seeing the flag flying.
2. Discuss the Battle of New Orleans, which was fought after the war ended. Discuss the boost it gave to national morale after a war that had been so poorly fought.

ESSAYS:

1. The Prophet persuaded people to follow him by using magic. We might think that strange, but to what extent do we rely on luck or good omens?
2. As an American in 1812, summarize the arguments you would give for going to war or for opposing going to war.
3. Looking back on the war in 1815, discuss whether it was a good idea or a bad idea. Support your opinion.

CHALLENGES:

1. Who became Speaker of the House in 1811?
2. Why was the *Chesapeake* Affair especially embarrassing to the United States?
3. What feat of magic did the Prophet perform? How did it help Tecumseh?
4. Who were the War Hawks? Why were they called that?
5. What was "impressment"?
6. What happened in 1803 that might explain part of the reason why Napoleon wanted to sell Louisiana in a hurry?
7. What situation did the Americans take advantage of during England's war with France?
8. What did Americans find at Tippecanoe that made them angry with the British?
9. Where was the peace treaty signed?
10. What future presidents became famous during the War of 1812?

NATIONAL STANDARDS CORRELATIONS:

NCSS VIf: (Power, Authority, & Governance) Explain conditions, actions, and motivations that contribute to conflict and cooperation within and among nations.
NSH Era 4, Standard 1: United States territorial expansion between 1801 and 1861, and how it affected relations with external powers and Native Americans

WEBSITES:

http://www.army.mil/cmh-pg/books/amh/amh-06.htm
"Chapter 6: The War of 1812," The United States Army

http://www.si.edu/resource/faq/nmah/starflag.htm
"Star-Spangled Banner and the War of 1812," Smithsonian Institute

http://www.yale.edu/lawweb/avalon/diplomacy/britain/br1814m.htm
"The War of 1812," The Avalon Project at Yale Law School

The Missouri Compromise Is Passed

Henry Clay

By 1820, America had grown from 13 states in 1790 to 22 states and from a population of under 4 million to 9.6 million. The area east of the Mississippi River was growing rapidly; in some states, the population doubled every ten years. The region west of the mighty river was also beginning to fill in as well. Missouri, with 19,000 people in 1810, had 66,000 in 1820. Missouri Territory applied for statehood in 1817, but no action was taken for two years. In 1819, Maine also wanted statehood, which kept a balance of slave and free states. When Congress passed an enabling act, state governments were to be formed by Maine and Missouri.

Then something simple became complicated. Representative James Tallmadge of New York wanted an amendment to the enabling legislation. He proposed that no more slaves be taken to Missouri, and those born of slave parents in the state would be freed at the age of twenty-five. Two issues were raised by that proposal. Did Congress have any right to tell Missouri that it had to accept statehood with strings attached? More important at the time was this new limitation on the future of slavery.

At the same time Missouri was being discussed, the Senate was debating the new Adams-Onis Treaty with Spain. By it, the United States acquired Florida but gave up any claim to Texas. Large areas might be opened to settlement in the northern regions of Louisiana, but no further growth would be possible for the South. Now Tallmadge was going to end slavery in Missouri sometime in the next 30 or 40 years. Many in the southern states had seen the faults of slavery and had labeled it a "necessary evil." Without slaves, they could not produce cotton, tobacco, or rice as cheaply as they could with slave labor. People in the southern states had never thought of themselves as a unit before, pulling together against outsiders. For the first time, the South rallied around slavery; instead of admitting that it was wrong, they defended it as a "positive good."

A compromise was offered by Senator Jesse Thomas of Illinois. By it, Missouri would enter the Union as a slave state, Maine as a free state, and the territories in the Louisiana Purchase north of 36°30' would be free. It barely passed. Then Missouri confused things again by writing a constitution that would prohibit free African-Americans from entering the state. Another hot debate took place in Congress, but Henry Clay worked out a deal. A resolution was passed saying that Missouri must never use its power to take away the rights of any American citizen. Missouri promised to abide by the rule and was admitted in August 1821.

RESULTS: The War of 1812 brought the nation together, and people were just beginning to think of themselves as Americans. For a time, there was only one political party. By 1820, however, the mood was changing. People of the South saw northerners as oppressors wanting to take away their rights. In the same way, people from western states saw themselves as different from easterners. The nation was moving toward deep divisions that would lead to a civil war 40 years later.

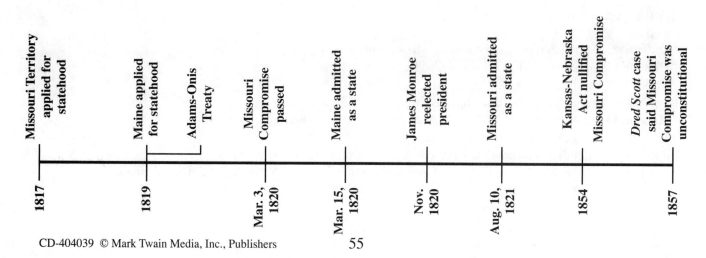

Missouri Territory applied for statehood — 1817

Maine applied for statehood — 1819

Adams-Onis Treaty

Missouri Compromise passed — Mar. 3, 1820

Maine admitted as a state — Mar. 15, 1820

James Monroe reelected president — Nov. 1820

Missouri admitted as a state — Aug. 10, 1821

Kansas-Nebraska Act nullified Missouri Compromise — 1854

Dred Scott case said Missouri Compromise was unconstitutional — 1857

Name: _____ Date: _____

The Missouri Compromise Is Passed: Reinforcement

Directions: Complete the following activities, essays, and challenges on your own paper.

ACTIVITIES:

1. Discuss how a simple problem can become complex by adding a condition on to it.
2. Discuss how people have a tendency to forget what the original issue is when they get angry. Slavery became the issue instead of whether Missouri and Maine should be states.

ESSAYS:

1. Summarize the Missouri Compromise and what it meant to the expansion of slavery. Do you feel it was a good arrangement for that time?
2. The idea of gradual emancipation (keeping all present slaves as slaves and freeing their children when they reached 25) had been used in some of the northern states. As a southern politician of the time, how would you have felt about that idea? Why?
3. Would you have considered James Tallmadge a troublemaker for raising the issue if you had been in Congress at the time? Why?

CHALLENGES:

1. What did people mean by slavery being a "necessary evil"?
2. What is an "enabling act"?
3. What other state would come in when Missouri did?
4. What was meant by the Missouri Compromise line?
5. Who proposed the Missouri Compromise? From which state did he come?
6. What area did the United States get in 1819? What area did the United States give up claim to in the Adams-Onís Treaty?
7. Who did Missouri try to keep out?
8. Look at a map of the Louisiana Purchase. Would the area open to slavery or the area closed to slavery be the larger?
9. How was the nation becoming divided regionally?
10. Why were the late 1810s and early 1820s known as the "Era of Good Feeling"?

NATIONAL STANDARDS CORRELATIONS:

NCSS VIc: (Power, Authority, & Governance) Analyze and explain ideas and governmental mechanisms to meet needs and wants of citizens, regulate territory, manage conflict, and establish order and security.
NSH Era 4, Standard 3: The extension, restriction, and reorganization of political democracy after 1800

WEBSITES:

http://www.loc.gov/rr/program/bib/ourdocs/Missouri.html
"Missouri Compromise," The Library of Congress

http://www.ourdocuments.gov/doc.php?flash=true&doc=22
"Missouri Compromise (1820)," The U.S. National Archives and Records Administration

http://www.digitalhistory.uh.edu/database/article_display.cfm?HHID=574
"The Era of Good Feelings: The Growth of Political Factionalism and Sectionalism," Digital History

The Election Where Second Place Was Good Enough to Win

John Q Adams

The writers of the Constitution had done an amazing job, but they could not predict everything that might happen in the future. An example of this occurred in 1800. Political parties had developed by then, and Jefferson and Burr tied in the electoral vote. The Constitution gave the House the job of picking a winner, and it chose Jefferson. To keep it from happening again, the Twelfth Amendment was passed. It said that the president and vice president were to be chosen by separate ballots. If no one had a majority of votes, the House of Representatives would choose the president from among the top three candidates, and the Senate would choose the vice president from the top two. No one at the time could have guessed how soon the Twelfth Amendment would be used to select a president.

In 1824, everyone knew that President Monroe's second term was coming to an end and there was only one political party. The Federalist party was dying out, and only a few were still active in politics. There were no political conventions or presidential primaries at that time. Instead, candidates were chosen by a caucus of party leaders in Congress who picked their choice for president. The caucus in 1824 chose William Crawford, the secretary of the treasury. However, most party leaders did not attend the caucus—they had their own candidates to run. Among these were Secretary of State John Quincy Adams, Speaker of the House Henry Clay, Secretary of War John C. Calhoun, and General Andrew Jackson. Each was from a different state, and only Adams was from New England.

Until this time, electors had all been chosen by the state legislatures, but a few states now allowed the voters to make the choice. They did choose the most popular candidate: Jackson (153,000), followed by Adams (108,000), Clay (47,000), and Crawford (46,000). In electoral votes, it came out as Jackson, Adams, Crawford, and Clay. No candidate had the majority of electoral votes. Since Clay was fourth, he was out of the running. But as Speaker of the House, he had great influence.

Crawford was not a possible choice. He had suffered a stroke, and, while he was on his way to recovery, his health problems could not be ignored. Both Jackson and Adams believed they should be chosen. Adams was well educated and had been a diplomat and an outstanding secretary of state. Jackson was a military hero who had served as a judge and briefly as a senator.

Clay went to Adams' house one night, and the two men talked for hours. Clay secretly decided that Adams was best for the job and applied pressure on members wavering between the two men. With Clay's help, Adams won the election, even though he was second in popular and in electoral votes. Jackson was angry and felt that he deserved the job. When Adams picked Clay to be Secretary of State, Jackson and his followers were sure a corrupt deal had been struck between Adams and Clay.

RESULTS: Adams was able to do little as president because Jackson supporters in Congress blocked him.

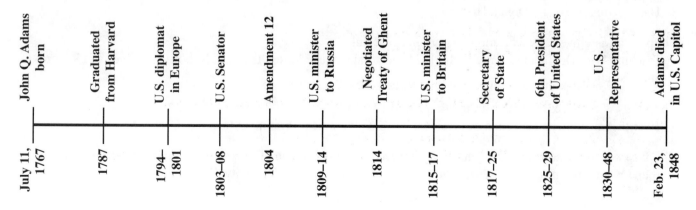

John Q. Adams born	Graduated from Harvard	U.S. diplomat in Europe	U.S. Senator	Amendment 12	U.S. minister to Russia	Negotiated Treaty of Ghent	U.S. minister to Britain	Secretary of State	6th President of United States	U.S. Representative	Adams died in U.S. Capitol
July 11, 1767	1787	1794–1801	1803–08	1804	1809–14	1814	1815–17	1817–25	1825–29	1830–48	Feb. 23, 1848

Name: _____ Date: _____

The Election Where Second Place Was Good Enough to Win: Reinforcement

Directions: Complete the following activities, essays, and challenges on your own paper.

ACTIVITIES:

1. Describe how the election process changed from caucus to convention to primary-chosen candidates.
2. Discuss the Electoral College and how the number of electors is determined.

ESSAYS:

1. For many years, the presidents had all been secretaries of state (Jefferson, Madison, Monroe, Adams). Do you think that a secretary of state would have more qualifications than a governor or senator might have?
2. If the caucus system were still in use, what would people say about it?
3. After researching John Q. Adams, do you think he would have any possibility of being elected president today? Why or why not?

CHALLENGES:

1. The Constitution said electors were to pick two candidates, and whichever one had the most votes would be president and the second-most would be vice president. How did the coming of political parties mess that up?
2. How did the Twelfth Amendment correct that problem?
3. Which candidates in 1824 were not in Monroe's Cabinet?
4. How many Americans (in round numbers) cast popular votes for president in 1824?
5. Did Jackson have a majority (more than half) of the votes cast in 1824, or did he have a plurality (more than anyone else had)?
6. Which candidates in 1824 were members of the Monroe Cabinet?
7. Why did Henry Clay and others not seriously consider Crawford?
8. If Jackson had heard of the secret meeting of Clay and Adams, what would he have thought about it?
9. How had presidential candidates been chosen before this time?
10. How successful was John Quincy Adams as president? Why?

NATIONAL STANDARDS CORRELATIONS:

NCSS VIb: (Power, Authority, & Governance) Describe the purpose of government and how its powers are acquired, used, and justified.
NSH Era 4, Standard 3: The extension, restriction, and reorganization of political democracy after 1800

WEBSITES:

http://www.digitalhistory.uh.edu/documents/documents_p2.cfm?doc=59
"The Election of 1824," Digital History

http://www.archives.gov/education/lessons/electoral-tally/
"Teaching With Documents: Tally of the 1824 Electoral College Vote," The U.S. National Archives and Records Administration

http://www.gpoaccess.gov/constitution/html/amdt12.html
"Twelfth Amendment—Election of President," U.S. Government Printing Office

http://www.americanpresident.org/history/johnquincyadams/biography/CampaignsElections.com.mon.shtml
"John Quincy Adams (1825–1829)," The Rector and Visitors of the University of Virginia

Americans Invest in Internal Improvements

Early Locomotive

The coming of the steamboat was only the beginning of a great change that occurred in America. Prior to 1800, Americans were plagued by slow transportation. Roads were often paths cut through the forest with stumps just low enough that a wagon could pass over them. Rivers were the main method of getting goods to market, but they could run low, flood, or have a current too swift at points for safe passage. The need for improvement to travel was obvious, and different approaches were used to accomplish it.

Construction began on the National Road in 1811; it was to be a turnpike built between Cumberland, Maryland, and Wheeling, Virginia. It was America's first superhighway, and it was completed in 1818. It was 30 feet wide in the mountains and 66 feet wide elsewhere. With solid bridges and a gravel base, it seemed like a work of wonder to travelers. By the 1830s, a trip from Washington to Wheeling took only thirty hours! Other privately owned turnpikes were built as well, but most roads continued to be very poor.

Another improvement was the Erie Canal. Built between Albany and Buffalo, New York, from 1817 to 1825, it was an enormous success. It was 364 miles long, four feet deep, and 40 feet wide. It carried the commerce of the Great Lakes to New York and made it the center of the nation's trade. For shippers, the cost dropped from 20 cents a ton mile to 2 cents. Other states also built canals, especially Ohio and Indiana, but theirs were never as successful as New York's. It did not take long for the canal era to end, however, as stiff new competition came from the railroad.

In the early 1820s, English inventors began to work on steam engines to do work, and Americans who were aware of this saw the potential of railroads for America. In 1828, construction began on the Baltimore & Ohio (B&O) Railroad, and in 1830, thirteen miles of it opened for business. Soon other railroads were being built in America.

Traveling by train was regarded as an almost foolhardy thing for a person to do. Sparks from the locomotive's boiler blew back on passengers, and since many boilers were poorly made, explosions occurred. Railroads put on barrier cars that were piled high with cotton between the locomotive and the train to protect the customers.

Improvements came very quickly. The "Tom Thumb," the first American-built locomotive on the B&O, had top speed of 15 mph, but averaged only 5.5 mph. In a race with a horse, it lost because of mechanical failures, but it proved itself in the long pull by hauling forty-two passengers with its 1.43 horsepower. In 1832, just two years after the "Tom Thumb" was built, the Mohawk and Hudson Railroad built the "Brother Jonathan," which was much heavier and more powerful. It could move at a top speed of 80 mph.

RESULTS: Americans quickly saw the importance of railroads, which could transport people far more rapidly than a stagecoach and in the winter when streams were frozen. Most railroads were constructed east-west, and this caused less contact between Northerners and Southerners. The North's railroads were far superior to those in the South, which would become a factor during the Civil War.

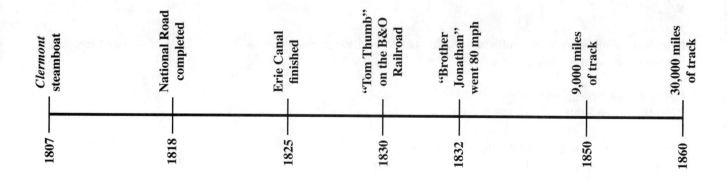

Clermont steamboat	National Road completed	Erie Canal finished	"Tom Thumb" on the B&O Railroad	"Brother Jonathan" went 80 mph	9,000 miles of track	30,000 miles of track
1807	1818	1825	1830	1832	1850	1860

Name: _____ Date: _____

Americans Invest in Internal Improvements: Reinforcement

Directions: Complete the following activities, essays, and challenges on your own paper.

ACTIVITIES:

1. Discuss how modern transportation has changed in much the same way this earlier change occurred.
2. If water transportation is cheaper than land transportation, discuss the advantages of land transportation.

ESSAYS:

1. As an investor, which would have appealed most to you as a way to make money: turnpikes, canals, or railroads? Why?
2. What is the effect of an invention on something that already exists? What kinds of examples help to prove your point?
3. A railroad wants to put a line by your town but requires that the town put up money for the station and right-of-way. What arguments would you hear for the town doing this?

CHALLENGES:

1. What is the other name by which the Cumberland Road was known?
2. How long was the stagecoach trip from Washington to Wheeling?
3. How much did the completion of the Erie Canal save shippers (per ton mile)?
4. What city was at the western end of the Erie Canal?
5. What was America's first railroad?
6. Why was railroad travel considered dangerous?
7. Why did the locomotive Tom Thumb lose a race with a horse?
8. If your lawnmower has a four-horsepower engine, how much more horsepower does it have than the Tom Thumb?
9. Why were railroads able to overtake the lead of canals?
10. How fast could the Brother Jonathan go at full speed?

NATIONAL STANDARDS CORRELATIONS:

NCSS VIIIa: (Science, Technology, & Society) Examine and describe the influence of culture on scientific and technological choices and advancement, such as in transportation, medicine, and warfare.
NSH Era 4, Standard 2: How the industrial revolution, increasing immigration, the rapid expansion of slavery, and the westward movement changed the lives of Americans and led toward regional tensions

WEBSITES:

http://americanhistory.si.edu/onthemove/exhibition/exhibition_1_1.html
"Transportation in America before 1876," Smithsonian Institute

http://www.nationalroadpa.org/
"The Road that Built the Nation," National Road Heritage Corridor

http://www.canals.state.ny.us/cculture/history/
"The Erie Canal: A Brief History," New York State Canals

A "Man Of the People" Is Elected President of the United States

By 1828, the nation had expanded to over 12 million people, and it was clear that the old political rule by an elite was coming to an end. States were beginning to trust the people now to select their own leaders, and that included letting them vote for presidential electors. The choices in 1828 were the current president, John Q. Adams—former secretary of state, ambassador, and son of the second president—or Andrew Jackson, who had risen from the lower class to become a military hero. Unlike previous contests, which tended to be dull, there was a battle for public support this time, and the nation would witness its first dirty campaign.

Andrew Jackson

Andrew Jackson was born in a South Carolina log cabin. His father died before he was born, and by the time he was fourteen, his mother had died. Jackson grew up wild but learned enough to become a lawyer. He headed for Nashville, Tennessee, and fell in love with Rachel Robards, a married woman. When they thought her husband had divorced her, they married. Two years later, they learned that a divorce had just been granted, so they remarried. Future political enemies would charge that she was a bigamist. Jackson had a quick temper and warned that anyone insulting his wife would pay for it. When a man made remarks about Mrs. Jackson in a bar, Jackson challenged him to a duel and killed him.

Jackson was elected general of the Tennessee militia, and during the War of 1812, he won a battle over the Creek Nation at Horseshoe Bend and the final battle of the war at New Orleans. In 1818, he invaded Spanish Florida, captured Pensacola, and hanged two British subjects. Some considered him a madman out of control, but to those who liked men of action, he was a hero. People began to talk about Jackson for president, and in 1824, he received a plurality of popular and electoral votes but lost. No one doubted that he would return in 1828. Since there was only one party, it split between the National Republicans, who backed J.Q. Adams, and the Democratic Republicans backing Jackson.

Jackson supporters charged that Adams had stolen the 1824 election and accused him of wasting public money on a billiard table. Adams' men charged that Jackson was an adulterer, had murdered innocent Native Americans at Horseshoe Bend, and had fought duels. After Mrs. Jackson learned of the attacks on her character in newspapers, she died. Jackson was convinced that she died of a broken heart and could never forgive the men responsible.

RESULTS: When the election results were in, Jackson won with 178–83 electoral votes and 647,000–508,000 popular votes. The Adams faction feared the worst from Jackson, and their fears seemed to come true when hundreds of backwoodsmen walked or rode all the way to Washington for the occasion. After the formal ceremonies, the frontiersmen walked over to the White House and crashed the reception given in honor of the new president. The carpets were stained, and china and glassware were broken. To Jackson's opponents, it seemed that the mob had taken over.

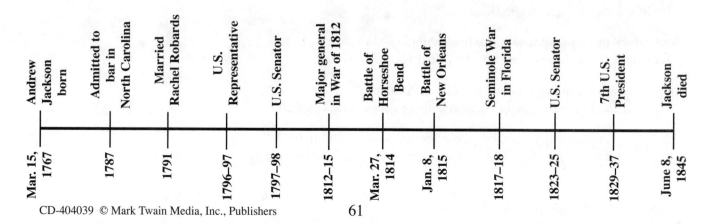

Andrew Jackson born	Mar. 15, 1767
Admitted to bar in North Carolina	1787
Married Rachel Robards	1791
U.S. Representative	1796–97
U.S. Senator	1797–98
Major general in War of 1812	1812–15
Battle of Horseshoe Bend	Mar. 27, 1814
Battle of New Orleans	Jan. 8, 1815
Seminole War in Florida	1817–18
U.S. Senator	1823–25
7th U.S. President	1829–37
Jackson died	June 8, 1845

Name: _____ Date: _____

A "Man Of the People" Is Elected
President of the United States: Reinforcement

Directions: Complete the following activities, essays, and challenges on your own paper.

ACTIVITIES:

1. Research Andrew Jackson, and decide if he would be considered a good candidate by modern voters today.
2. Discuss whether mudslinging helps or hurts the political process. Why?

ESSAYS:

1. Why do you think that elections often result in wild accusations? Do you think it is fair to bring up something that happened years ago? Why?
2. The "log cabin" candidate became a popular image. Do you think a person should be elected because he was poor and made good? Why?
3. Why were National Republicans so worried about what would happen when Jackson came into office that John Quincy Adams left town before the inauguration?

CHALLENGES:

1. In what state was Jackson born? With which state is he usually associated?
2. With which two battles in the War of 1812 was Jackson's name most associated?
3. Bigamy is being married to two people at the same time. How could that charge have been leveled at Mrs. Jackson?
4. Jackson's invasion of Florida raised problems with which two countries?
5. Which part of the Republican party backed Adams? Jackson?
6. What did the Jackson people accuse Adams of doing?
7. What did Adams' people accuse Jackson of doing?
8. By how many electoral votes did Jackson win in 1828?
9. What was unusual about the inauguration of Jackson?
10. What did Jackson enemies think of the reception?

NATIONAL STANDARDS CORRELATIONS:

NCSS Xf: (Civic Ideals & Practices) Identify and explain the roles of formal and informal political actors in influencing and shaping public policy and decision-making.
NSH Era 4, Standard 3: The extension, restriction, and reorganization of political democracy after 1800

WEBSITES:

http://www.whitehouse.gov/history/presidents/aj7.html
"Andrew Jackson," The White House

http://www.thehermitage.com/indexHouse.htm
"Biography," The Ladies Hermitage Association

http://www.yale.edu/lawweb/avalon/presiden/jackpap.htm
"The Papers of Andrew Jackson," The Avalon Project at Yale Law School

http://www.digitalhistory.uh.edu/database/article_display.cfm?HHID=637
"The Presidency of Andrew Jackson: The Election of 1828," Digital History

The Five Civilized Tribes Are Moved West

Osceola

The Native Americans in the United States were coming under increasing pressure in the 1820s. The small northern tribes were forced to leave valuable lands and were relocated to lands considered worthless. Meaningless treaties were signed by chiefs, and all tribal members were expelled. The southern tribes were larger and more organized, however. Known as the Five Civilized Tribes, they included Cherokees, Creeks, Chickasaws, Choctaws, and Seminoles. The largest was the Cherokee nation, which had adopted many of the white man's customs: religion, houses, clothing, and even slaveholding. A Cherokee named Sequoyah was so impressed with the "talking leaves" (written words) of the white man that he developed a written alphabet using the 85 syllables in his language. About the only major difference between whites and Native Americans was that the Native Americans took baths more often.

Whites were jealous of the Native Americans, who lived on valuable cotton lands that they wanted for themselves. President James Monroe resisted efforts to force the Native Americans to leave their homes, and J.Q. Adams turned down a treaty signed by some Creek chiefs that was very unpopular with most tribal members. Governor George Troup of Georgia was furious with this decision and began pressuring the Native Americans to leave, regardless of what the president thought.

Andrew Jackson had fought Native Americans and had little patience with their problems. It seemed to him they would be better off away from whites, and some Native Americans agreed. Tribes had often split on this issue. In 1825, Chief William McIntosh, a Chickasaw leader, signed a treaty giving up tribal lands, and Chief Menewa and his soldiers killed McIntosh. Later, Menewa joined the whites as they tried to remove the Seminoles. He hoped that it would save his people from being evicted, but it did not work, and he joined the long line of Chickasaws heading for Indian Territory.

Choctaw removal in 1831 was slowed by ice on the Mississippi River and heavy snows in the Arkansas swamps through which they passed. Desperately short on food, many starved while the man who was supposed to supply them stayed at home in Nashville because it was too cold to travel.

The Cherokees fought removal in the courts, and the Supreme Court agreed that their treaty rights had been violated, but Jackson refused to support the verdict of the Court. He was said to have remarked, "John Marshall has made his decision; now let him enforce it." The Cherokees were forced to leave, but some escaped to the mountains of North Carolina, where their descendants still live. The rest walked the "Trail of Tears," and many of them died on their way to Indian Territory.

Seminoles hid in Florida's swamps. Led by Chief Osceola, they stubbornly refused to move out. Mothers killed their children so they could fight by the sides of their husbands.

There were critics, like Henry Clay, who protested what was being done, but they had little impact on Jackson or his popularity.

RESULTS: Native Americans had a new homeland in what is now eastern Oklahoma, but they could never forget the suffering of their ancestors.

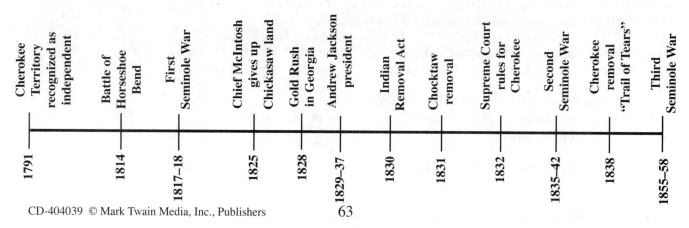

Cherokee Territory recognized as independent	Battle of Horseshoe Bend	First Seminole War	Chief McIntosh gives up Chickasaw land	Gold Rush in Georgia	Andrew Jackson president	Indian Removal Act	Chocktaw removal	Supreme Court rules for Cherokee	Second Seminole War	Cherokee removal "Trail of Tears"	Third Seminole War
1791	1814	1817–18	1825	1828	1829–37	1830	1831	1832	1835–42	1838	1855–58

Name: _____ Date: _____

The Five Civilized Tribes Are Moved West: Reinforcement

Directions: Complete the following activities, essays, and challenges on your own paper.

ACTIVITIES:

1. Discuss the problems that often happen between races and cultures. Research and find examples of this in Australia, South America, and South Africa, as well as in the United States.
2. Have the students look up individual tribes and the difficulties they suffered because of the Indian Removal Act.

ESSAYS:

1. Do you think removing Native Americans from their land, if it had been done without causing suffering, would have been justified? Why?
2. As a Native American living at that time, write your opinion about what has happened to you and your people.
3. What were some signs that the Native Americans were as civilized as their white neighbors?

CHALLENGES:

1. Why was it easier to move northern tribes than the Five Civilized Tribes?
2. What member of the Cherokee tribe put the Cherokee language into writing? How did he do it?
3. Name the Five Civilized Tribes.
4. Who opposed President J.Q. Adams' policy toward Native Americans?
5. What Chickasaw chief gave up tribal lands in the East, and what happened to him?
6. Why did the Choctaw suffer so much on their trip west?
7. What Seminole chief led the resistance to moving?
8. What was meant by Jackson's remark: "John Marshall has made his decision; now let him enforce it"?
9. What state was formed out of "Indian Territory"?
10. If you were to see a reenactment of the Trail of Tears, what tribe would be the center of attention?

NATIONAL STANDARDS CORRELATIONS:

NCSS IIIh: (People, Places, & Environments) Examine, interpret, and analyze physical and cultural patterns and their interactions, such as land use, settlement patterns, cultural transmission of customs and ideas, and ecosystem changes.

NSH Era 4, Standard 1: United States territorial expansion between 1801 and 1861, and how it affected relations with external powers and Native Americans

WEBSITES:

http://www.digitalhistory.uh.edu/database/article_display.cfm?HHID=638
"Jacksonian Democracy: Indian Removal," Digital History

http://memory.loc.gov/cgi-bin/ampage?collId=11s1&fileName=004/11s1004.db&recNum=458
"Statutes at Large, 21st Congress, 1st Session, Page 411," The Library of Congress

http://www.ourdocuments.gov/doc.php?flash=true&doc=25
"President Andrew Jackson's Message to Congress 'On Indian Removal' (1830)," The U.S. National Archives and Records Administration

http://www.pbs.org/wgbh/aia/part4/4p2959.html
"Indian Removal," Public Broadcasting Service

Jackson Declares War on Nullifiers and the Second Bank of the United States

President Jackson was a man with strong opinions on many issues, and rather than argue forever about what should be done, he acted. He had reacted strongly when Vice President John C. Calhoun of South Carolina said states had a right to cancel any law passed by Congress if it was unconstitutional (nullification). This would make the states more important than the federal government, and they could decide whether or not to obey a law. At the Jefferson birthday dinner in 1830, President Jackson looked across the table at Calhoun and offered a toast: "To the federal Union, it must be preserved." In 1833, South Carolina said it would nullify the tariff passed in 1832. Jackson warned that he would send an army against the state, and few doubted he would do it. South Carolina backed down.

Nicholas Biddle

If Jackson disagreed with Calhoun, he was even more angry with Nicholas Biddle, president of the Second Bank of the United States. Government banks were nothing new. England, France, and most European countries had a central bank. The United States had created the First Bank of the United States in 1791, but it was never popular with Republicans. Its charter expired in 1811, and Congress had not renewed it. By 1816, that was seen as a mistake, and the Second Bank was chartered for 20 years. There were good reasons to have the bank. It made it easy for the government to borrow money and gave it a safe place to deposit money. It also kept an eye on state banks and kept them from lending more money than they should.

There were also problems with the Bank, however. There was too much power in the hands of Biddle. He was the only member of its board who understood what it was doing. It also lent money to leading political leaders and did not worry about how quickly they paid it back. The Bank bought ads in newspapers, and the owners of the newspapers knew that they were required to write articles friendly to the Bank, or they would lose the advertising. State banks did not like the Second Bank and thought it interfered with their ability to loan money to risky customers. President Jackson didn't like banks, which could mean trouble when the bank asked for a new charter.

Many political leaders in 1832 considered Jackson high-handed and wanted Henry Clay to run as the National Republican candidate. Clay and Daniel Webster persuaded Biddle to ask for his bank charter in 1832, rather than wait four years. That way, the Bank would become the main issue in the campaign. A bill to recharter the Bank passed in Congress, but Jackson vetoed it, saying the Bank let the rich use the government for selfish purposes.

RESULTS: Jackson easily won the election and began to kill the Bank immediately. He withdrew government funds when he paid its bills. When money came in from taxes, it was placed in state banks. When its charter expired, the Second Bank was chartered as a Pennsylvania bank, but it did not last long and closed permanently in 1841.

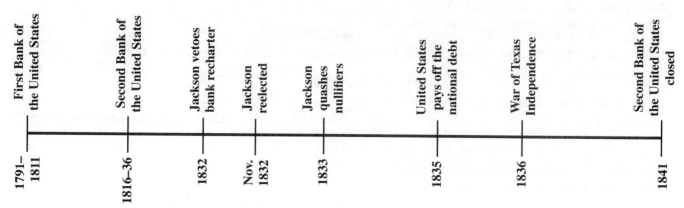

First Bank of the United States	Second Bank of the United States	Jackson vetoes bank recharter	Jackson reelected	Jackson quashes nullifiers	United States pays off the national debt	War of Texas Independence	Second Bank of the United States closed
1791–1811	1816–36	1832	Nov. 1832	1833	1835	1836	1841

Name: _____ Date: _____

Jackson Declares War on Nullifiers and the Second Bank of the United States: Reinforcement

Directions: Complete the following activities, essays, and challenges on your own paper.

ACTIVITIES:

1. Discuss what would happen today if any state could decide which federal laws it would obey and which it would disregard.
2. Discuss the problem with a bank (or any other powerful business) having too much influence on government.

ESSAYS:

1. Do you think nullification would create serious problems for the United States today? Why?
2. Review the reasons why the Bank should have been rechartered and why it should not have been. On which side would you have been in 1832? Why?
3. Congress approved the recharter of the Bank, and Jackson vetoed it. Do you think the president or Congress best represents the interests of the average American today? Why or why not?

CHALLENGES:

1. What was "nullification"?
2. What did Jackson threaten to do to South Carolina?
3. What are the main purposes for banks?
4. What were some good reasons for keeping the Second Bank?
5. Why was the Bank unpopular?
6. Who was president of the Second Bank of the United States?
7. Who suggested to the Bank's president that he should ask for the recharter in 1832?
8. What party opposed Jackson in the 1832 election?
9. How did Jackson weaken the Bank before its charter ran out?
10. What happened to the Second Bank after 1836?

NATIONAL STANDARDS CORRELATIONS:

NCSS VIIf: (Production, Distribution, & Consumption) Explain and illustrate how values and beliefs influence different economic decisions.
NSH Era 4, Standard 3: The extension, restriction, and reorganization of political democracy after 1800

WEBSITES:

http://www.digitalhistory.uh.edu/database/article_display.cfm?HHID=639
"Jacksonian Democracy: Nullification," Digital History

http://www.loc.gov/rr/program/bib/ourdocs/Nullification.html
"Nullification Proclamation," The Library of Congress

http://www.cr.nps.gov/history/online_books/butowsky2/constitution7.htm
"Second Bank of the United States," National Park Service

Some Slaves Refuse to Give in to Their Masters

Frederick Douglass

Since 1619, slavery had existed in the South, but when the Constitution was signed, it was agreed that the African slave trade would end within 20 years. A few hundred slaves were brought in illegally after 1808, but nearly all of the U.S. slaves had arrived or were born in America by that time. It is hard to say how slaves were treated because some masters were kind, while others were cruel. Some general things can be said. Masters bought slaves because there was work to be done, and few free laborers were willing to do that kind of work. Many slaves worked on plantations under white supervisors called "overseers" or black supervisors called "drivers." Most worked as "field hands," but others were servants or skilled laborers. Even though there were laws against teaching slaves to read, some were taught.

At best, slaves lived very insecure lives. A husband or wife might be sold by the master, and would never see each other again. Children belonged to the mother's master and could be sold. A kindly master might die, and they could find themselves with a cruel master. Even when things were going well, a slave worried. Masters added to that worry when they threatened to sell them "downriver"—a reminder that no matter how bad things might be where you are, it could be far worse somewhere else.

Some slaves never gave their masters any trouble. They did their work, and they found pleasure in their religion and in family and friends. Religion was important because it told them that a better day was coming, when they could go to heaven and be with God. Others found little ways to get even on earth: break a hoe, loaf on the job, steal food, or set fires. Sometimes they openly defied their masters, either in groups or as individuals.

Occasionally, there were large-scale slave revolts. In 1800, Gabriel's Revolt took place in Richmond. Gabriel, a blacksmith who could read, planned with other slaves to capture the arsenal and kidnap the governor; then other slaves would join them. Some slaves told their masters, and those involved in the plot were arrested; 20 were killed. In 1822, Denmark Vesey, a free black in Charleston, South Carolina, organized about 80 men; but again, slaves told their masters, and the group was crushed. Vesey and 34 others were tried and executed. The largest rebellion was that of Nat Turner in rural Southampton County, Virginia. Turner was convinced that God had chosen him to lead a rebellion, and he and his followers killed about 60 whites before they were captured, tried, and executed.

The story of Frederick Douglass is different. He was a slave in Maryland. His master tired of Frederick's allowing his horse to run away and decided to send him to Mr. Covey, an evil slave-breaker. After six months of brutal treatment, Douglass had had enough. In a long, two-hour wrestling match with Covey, Douglass came out on top. Covey never whipped him again. Later, Douglass escaped slavery and became an outstanding spokesman for the anti-slavery movement.

RESULTS: What slaves could or could not do was limited by the type of master they had. When the master understood that happy workers were more productive, slaves lived better; if the master felt harsh discipline was the only way to treat them, their lives were miserable.

Slaves developed methods of resistance that evened the score with the system that held them down. The Veseys and Turners were few in number, but their mere existence was enough to cause white concern.

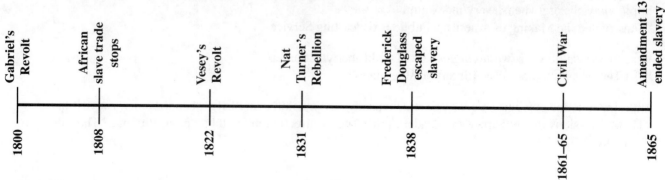

Gabriel's Revolt	African slave trade stops	Vesey's Revolt	Nat Turner's Rebellion	Frederick Douglass escaped slavery	Civil War	Amendment 13 ended slavery
1800	1808	1822	1831	1838	1861–65	1865

Name: _____ Date: _____

Some Slaves Refuse to Give in to Their Masters: Reinforcement

Directions: Complete the following activities, essays, and challenges on your own paper.

ACTIVITIES:

1. Discuss why more slaves did not openly rebel against their masters.
2. Discuss how rebellions caused more restrictions on slaves that, in turn, made it more difficult for them to get an education or move around.

ESSAYS:

1. All four African Americans mentioned (Gabriel, Vesey, Turner, and Douglass) had learned to read. Do you think that was important in what they did? Why?
2. Write about what you think it would have been like to be a slave. How do you think you would have handled the problems of the slaves?
3. Do you think open slave revolts were the best form of resistance? Why?

CHALLENGES:

1. When did the African slave trade end?
2. What were African-American supervisors called? White supervisors?
3. What job did most slaves have? What were some of the other jobs they had?
4. Why were slaves nervous, even when they had good masters?
5. Why were slaves so religious?
6. What two southern cities were threatened by major slave revolts?
7. Who planned to kidnap Governor James Monroe as part of his plot?
8. What were some ways in which slaves got even with unpopular masters when they did not want to risk an open revolt?
9. Who led the slave revolt that came closest to success?
10. How did Douglass handle his problem with Covey?

NATIONAL STANDARDS CORRELATIONS:

NCSS Id: (Culture) Explain why individuals and groups respond differently to their physical and social environments and/or changes to them on the basis of shared assumptions, values, and beliefs.

NSH Era 4, Standard 2: How the industrial revolution, increasing immigration, the rapid expansion of slavery, and the westward movement changed the lives of Americans and led toward regional tensions

WEBSITES:

http://www.liu.edu/cwis/cwp/library/aaslavry.htm
"The African American: A Journey from Slavery to Freedom," Long Island University

http://www.pbs.org/wnet/slavery/index.html
"Slavery and the Making of America," Public Broadcasting Service

http://www.lva.lib.va.us/whoweare/exhibits/DeathLiberty/natturner/
"Nat Turner's Rebellion," The Library of Virginia

http://memory.loc.gov/cgi-bin/query/r?ammem/aaodyssey:@field(NUMBER+@band(rbcmisc+ody0108()
"The Confessions of Nat Turner, the Leader of the Late Insurrection in Southhampton, Virginia," The Library of Congress

The North Develops an Industrial Economy

Thomas Jefferson had dreamed of an agricultural nation, with each man working for himself. That idea was still strong in the South in 1840 but was losing out in the Northeast. Factories developed, especially in New England where land was poor and fast-flowing streams produced water power capable of running machines. Textile mills were built, and that opened job opportunities. As transportation improved, anything produced in a Rhode Island factory could be sold anywhere in the United States or Europe.

New inventions came along, increasing the need for factories. In 1810, there were only 77 patents issued, but in 1830, 544 were issued. New products meant more jobs and more factories. Companies were formed. Sometimes they had only one owner; others were corporations with stockholders. In small companies, the company president knew the employees; but as companies got larger, they became more impersonal.

Early textile mills are a good example. New England towns worried that unless they created jobs, the young people would leave, so they built a mill to employ local workers. Girls came to the factory with their fathers, who wanted to know that their daughters would be safe. The factory owner assured each father that the girl would be supervised; he kept a boardinghouse for the girls to live in. For the girls, this was a way to leave home and live on their own for a time before they married. Many lived on farms and knew few boys, so they also hoped for an opportunity to meet young men.

Young Lady Working in Textile Mill

Factories at first tried to make the setting as homey as possible. Flowers were put on window ledges, and little sayings from Ben Franklin or the Bible might be on the equipment for the girls to read and think about during the day. Lecturers were sometimes brought in to give speeches. A pleasant and moral atmosphere was what they wanted.

Each day, the girls would be awakened by a bell, eat breakfast, march to the mill, and work about 12 hours. In the evening, the girls marched back to the boardinghouse, ate supper, and were in bed by 9 p.m. It did not take long for them to tire of this routine, and soon there were vacancies at the mill. Others worked there too. Child labor was common, with boys and girls eight years old and up working 10 to 12 hours a day. Families were sometimes hired. All of this meant little chance for children to attend school.

As the factory got larger, new workers were hired from England, Ireland, or Europe. Most of these young workers were girls who had little education, and some of whom spoke no English. Factory owners were now less interested in caring for the workers and more interested in making money. They took away the flower boxes and the sayings.

RESULTS: Some workers tried to form unions, but they were not popular with the public at the time and were often declared illegal by the courts. Workers knew that newly arrived immigrants would gladly replace them on their jobs, so they were in a poor position to demand higher wages or shorter hours. Despite problems, the American factory workers were better treated than those in Europe.

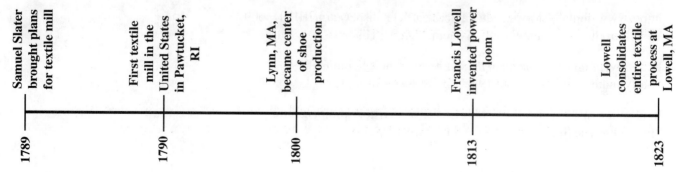

1789	1790	1800	1813	1823
Samuel Slater brought plans for textile mill	First textile mill in the United States in Pawtucket, RI	Lynn, MA, became center of shoe production	Francis Lowell invented power loom	Lowell consolidates entire textile process at Lowell, MA

Name: _____ Date: _____

The North Develops an Industrial Economy: Reinforcement

Directions: Complete the following activities, essays, and challenges on your own paper.

ACTIVITIES:

1. Have students discuss what would happen if a new, low-skill factory started in their town. What would happen to employment, housing costs, and jobs in other businesses in the community?
2. Have students look up pre-Civil War inventors like Samuel Colt, Samuel F. B. Morse, Charles Goodyear, and Francis Lowell. What was the impact of their discoveries?

ESSAYS:

1. Discuss how your life would be different if you had lived in the 1830s and had worked in one of these factories.
2. The prices for cloth dropped because of factories. Do you think the person who bought the cloth worried about the worker who produced it? Why?
3. What inventions can you think of that have created jobs today? How are modern workers in those factories alike and different from those who worked in factories before the Civil War?

CHALLENGES:

1. How did inventions affect job opportunities?
2. What kind of people were often hired to work in the first textile mills?
3. Why were boardinghouses often provided by the mill owners?
4. How young were some of the workers? How much education did they get?
5. Why was New England the center of much of textile production?
6. Why did the young women who worked at these factories grow unhappy with their jobs?
7. From where were new workers recruited?
8. Why didn't workers strike more than they did?
9. Why were flower boxes removed, and why were other efforts to provide homey surroundings discontinued?
10. The South had very few textile mills until later. What do you think the southern farmer thought about conditions in the mills?

NATIONAL STANDARDS CORRELATIONS:

NCSS VIIa: (Production, Distribution, & Consumption) Give and explain examples of ways that economic systems structure choices about how goods and services are to be produced and distributed.
NSH Era 4, Standard 2: How the industrial revolution, increasing immigration, the rapid expansion of slavery, and the westward movement changed the lives of Americans and led toward regional tensions

WEBSITES:

http://www.digitalhistory.uh.edu/database/article_display.cfm?HHID=609
"The Introduction of the Factory System," Digital History

http://invention.smithsonian.org/centerpieces/whole_cloth/u2ei/
"Early Industrialization: Unit Two," Smithsonian Institute

http://www.nps.gov/lowe/loweweb/Lowell%20History/prologue.htm
"Prologue: The Spirit of the Past," National Park Service

Houston Leads Texans to Independence

Sam Houston

In the early 1830s, Texas was still part of Mexico, but its people were much different from those south of the Rio Grande. Texas had been a neglected part of Spanish territory until the Mexicans gained freedom. In 1820, Moses Austin had an idea of bringing American Catholic settlers into Texas, but he died before it could be arranged. His son, Stephen Austin, followed through with his idea, and in 1823 the terms were accepted. He was to settle 300 Catholic families in Texas. Each family would receive 177 acres for farming and 13,100 acres of grazing land. Austin would receive $1 for each eight acres of land, and when 200 families had come in, he got a bonus of 65,000 acres. Other colonies were established as well, but Austin's was the largest and most important.

Sam Houston was one of the people who came to Texas. His family had moved from Virginia to Tennessee, but he did not like the farmwork. So, he left home and went to live with the Cherokee. During the War of 1812, he was in Jackson's army at the Battle of Horseshoe Bend and was badly wounded. After the war, he became a lawyer and was elected governor of Tennessee. When he and his wife broke up, he resigned as governor and went back to live with the Cherokee. In 1832, he went to Texas.

By 1835, relations between Texas and Mexico were very bad, which led to a revolution. The first battles were disasters for the Texans. General Santa Anna surrounded the defenders of the Alamo, who fought to the last man. At Goliad, the Texans were defeated again. The Texans turned to Sam Houston to be their leader; however, Houston's strategy bothered many. He retreated and burned fields so that Santa Anna's army would have to bring up all their supplies. While he moved back, he trained his men so that when the time was right, they would be ready to win.

It was at San Jacinto Creek that Houston decided to attack. His men charged Santa Anna's camp, shouting "Remember the Alamo," and "Remember Goliad." They won a quick victory. Prisoners were rounded up, but they could not find Santa Anna. Two days later, he was discovered in a corporal's uniform. Since he had been president of Mexico, Houston forced him to sign a statement giving Texas its independence. After Santa Anna was released, he said he had no authority to give Texas independence, and it was still part of Mexico; also, the boundary of Texas was in dispute. Mexico said Texas was the region north of the Nueces River, while Texans claimed the land south to the Rio Grande.

RESULTS: The next few years were hard on Texas. It wanted to be part of the United States, but many northern politicians did not want Texas because it allowed slavery. Texas was recognized as independent by England, France, and the United States, but it lived under the threat that Mexico would send an army against it. It was not until after James Polk was elected U.S. president in 1844, that progress was made. Because Polk supported expansion into Texas, the outgoing president, John Tyler, pushed through a joint resolution admitting Texas to the Union. Mexico was angry and did not accept this as the final word. The issue of Texas and the boundary would be settled by war.

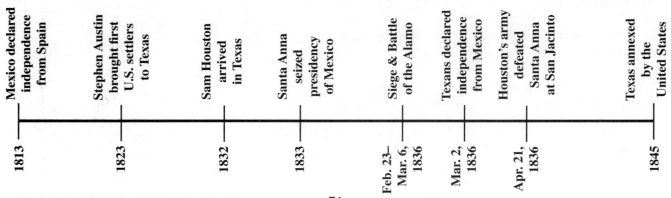

Mexico declared independence from Spain	Stephen Austin brought first U.S. settlers to Texas	Sam Houston arrived in Texas	Santa Anna seized presidency of Mexico	Siege & Battle of the Alamo	Texans declared independence from Mexico	Houston's army defeated Santa Anna at San Jacinto	Texas annexed by the United States
1813	1823	1832	1833	Feb. 23– Mar. 6, 1836	Mar. 2, 1836	Apr. 21, 1836	1845

Name: _____ Date: _____

Houston Leads Texans to Independence: Reinforcement

Directions: Complete the following activities, essays, and challenges on your own paper.

ACTIVITIES:

1. Look at a map of Texas and identify the location of San Antonio, the Rio Grande, the Nueces River, and Houston.
2. Create a time line for Sam Houston's life, listing the key events.

ESSAYS:

1. What was there about Sam Houston that made him a good military commander?
2. The Republic of Texas had a hard time financing its government. Why do you think people were not anxious to buy Texas bonds?

CHALLENGES:

1. Which American got the idea of colonizing Texas?
2. How many acres of land did settlers receive?
3. With which Native American tribe did Houston live twice?
4. At what battle was Sam Houston wounded?
5. What were the early battles that Texans lost?
6. What disputes did Mexico and Texas have over borders?
7. Why was the United States slow to bring Texas into the Union?
8. What countries recognized Texas as being independent besides the United States?
9. How was Texas admitted to the Union?
10. Who was U.S. president when Texas was admitted?

NATIONAL STANDARDS CORRELATIONS:

NCSS VIc: (Power, Authority, & Governance) Analyze and explain ideas and governmental mechanisms to meet needs and wants of citizens, regulate territory, manage conflict, and establish order and security.
NSH Era 4, Standard 1: United States territorial expansion between 1801 and 1861, and how it affected relations with external powers and Native Americans

WEBSITES:

http://www.tsha.utexas.edu/handbook/online/articles/HH/fho73.html
"Houston, Samuel, (1793–1863)," The Handbook of Texas Online

http://www.tsl.state.tx.us/treasures/giants/houston-01.html
"Sam Houston," Texas State Library and Archives Commission

http://www.thealamo.org/main.html
"The Alamo," Daughters of the Republic of Texas, Inc.

Americans Take an Interest in Oregon

John Jacob Astor

Even before Lewis and Clark went to Oregon in 1805, there was an American presence there. Captain Robert Gray went to Oregon in 1787 and took a load of sea otters that he had killed there to China. He returned in 1791 and discovered a river that he named after his ship, the *Columbia*. There was a fortune to be made in Oregon, and one shipowner made $20,000 from furs he bought from the Native Americans for $2 worth of trinkets. John Jacob Astor established a fort in Oregon in 1811, that he named Astoria. It was sold to the Northwest Company, a British firm, which merged with Hudson's Bay Company in 1821. Hudson's Bay sent Dr. John McLoughlin to Oregon to take over its land operations, but American ships still used the coast. In fact, so many of these were New England-owned, that the Native Americans referred to all white men as "Bostons."

American interest in Oregon grew very slowly, almost one man at a time. Dr. John Floyd of Virginia was a member of Congress who wanted the United States to annex it. Most people laughed at him. They said Oregon was too far away and that the natural boundary for the United States was the Rocky Mountains. The government was not going to act; however, private individuals did.

Hall Kelley was a Massachusetts schoolteacher who became excited over Oregon after he read the *Journal of Lewis and Clark*. After years of talking about Oregon, he went to Mexico, then through California, and on to Oregon. The governor of California did not trust him and sent a letter to McLoughlin accusing Kelley of being a cattle thief. Kelley did little in Oregon, but when he returned, he talked about what a marvelous place it was. One of those listening was Nathaniel Wyeth, who made two trips there.

Missionaries were interested in converting the Native Americans. Jason and Daniel Lee went as Methodist missionaries; Samuel Parker, Dr. Marcus Whitman, and Henry Spalding were Presbyterian missionaries; and Father De Smet went as a Catholic missionary. The journey of Dr. Whitman and Reverend Spalding was especially important because they brought their wives with them. It had always been thought that an overland journey was too hard for a woman to make, but that theory was proven wrong.

Enthusiasm for Oregon grew rapidly in the early 1840s. Many Americans wanted to go there because of free land, a sense of adventure, and a desire to make Oregon part of the United States. In 1843, a large wagon train of 1,000 people headed west from Independence, Missouri. Those who brought herds of cattle and oxen traveled too slowly for those who took only necessities, so the group divided between the light column and cow column.

The trip was never easy, but there were some things a group could do to improve their chances of a successful journey: (1) Have good leaders and listen to them. (2) Have good teams of oxen, mules, or horses, and have a sturdy wagon. (3) It helped to travel light. Many pioneers overloaded the wagons, and when the team got tired, they had to throw off unneeded items. Discarded dishes, tables, clothes, etc., littered the trail.

RESULTS: The United States and England agreed in 1846 to divide the line between the United States and Canada at the 49th parallel.

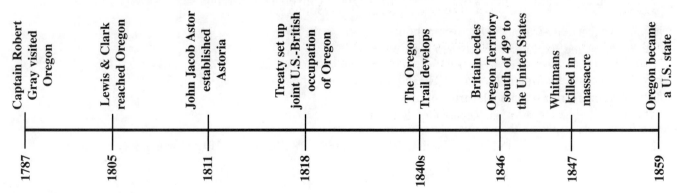

1787	1805	1811	1818	1840s	1846	1847	1859
Captain Robert Gray visited Oregon	Lewis & Clark reached Oregon	John Jacob Astor established Astoria	Treaty set up joint U.S.-British occupation of Oregon	The Oregon Trail develops	Britain cedes Oregon Territory south of 49° to the United States	Whitmans killed in massacre	Oregon became a U.S. state

Name: _____ Date: _____

Americans Take an Interest in Oregon: Reinforcement

Directions: Complete the following activities, essays, and challenges on your own paper.

ACTIVITIES:

1. Examine a map of Oregon as it was in the 1840s. Ask what states were formed from Oregon Country.
2. Research geographic information about Oregon and discuss how rainfall, mountains, rivers, etc., have affected life in Oregon.

ESSAYS:

1. You are planning a trip to Oregon in the near future. What advice given to those going in the 1840s would still be useful?
2. After looking at a map showing the Oregon Trail, what were some of the major rivers, stop-off points, and landmarks?
3. Describe the problems that would have been faced by those going to Oregon.

CHALLENGES:

1. Who was the first American to travel to Oregon?
2. For what company did Dr. John McLoughlin work?
3. What encouraged Hall Kelley to go to Oregon?
4. What two missionaries took their wives to Oregon?
5. Where did the 1843 caravan organize for the trip to Oregon?
6. What was the name of Gray's ship? Why was that important?
7. Why did Native Americans call the sailors "Bostons"?
8. Why was McLoughlin suspicious of Kelley?
9. What were some important things for travelers to do as they prepared to go overland to Oregon?
10. Where was the boundary line established between Oregon and Canada?

NATIONAL STANDARDS CORRELATIONS:

NCSS IIIh: (People, Places, & Environments) Examine, interpret, and analyze physical and cultural patterns and their interactions, such as land use, settlement patterns, cultural transmission of customs and ideas, and ecosystem changes.

NSH Era 4, Standard 2: How the industrial revolution, increasing immigration, the rapid expansion of slavery, and the westward movement changed the lives of Americans and led toward regional tensions

WEBSITES:

http://xroads.virginia.edu/~HYPER/HNS/Mtmen/home.html
"The Mountain Men: Pathfinders of the West, 1810–1860," University of Virginia

http://www.isu.edu/~trinmich/Discoverers.html
"Discoverers and Explorers," Boettcher/Trinklein Inc.

http://www.state.gov/r/pa/ho/time/dwe/16335.htm
"The Oregon Territory," U.S. Department of State

http://www.pbs.org/weta/thewest/people/s_z/whitman.htm
"Marcus Whitman (1802–1847) and Narcissa Whitman (1808–1847)," Public Broadcasting Service

Abolitionists Act, Congress Reacts

William Lloyd Garrison

One feature of the American character is the desire to reform everyone else. It is also American for those criticized to complain that the reformers have no proof for the charges, and they are troublemakers trying to disrupt the life of the individual or even the nation.

Many reformers were part of pre-Civil War America. Horace Mann pushed for tax-supported public education; critics said it was too expensive. He won, and by 1860, all northern states had public school. Some women and a few men favored giving women the vote; they did not win. Dorothea Dix brought about better treatment for the insane. Dr. Elizabeth Blackwell, America's first woman physician, was proof that women could survive in the professional world. Some said society was beyond hope and formed idealistic communities like Brook Farm in Massachusetts, New Harmony in Indiana, and Oneida in New York.

Of all reformers, none were as unpopular as abolitionists. Their goal was to end slavery, everywhere and immediately. Many admitted slavery was wrong, including some southerners, but abolitionists were more than against slavery—they wanted to destroy it and make slave-owners suffer for their terrible deeds against slaves. Many in the North did not share their views, however; they wanted southern products like cotton and tobacco and knew they would be hard to produce without slaves. They also felt that slavery was no harder than conditions in northern factories. They argued that southern states should be left alone to work out their own policies.

The first critics of slavery were Quakers, but most did little more than say it was wrong. Samuel Cornish and John Russwurm, free African Americans, published the first African-American-owned newspaper, *Freedom's Journal,* in 1827. A Quaker named Benjamin Lundy published *The Genius of Universal Emancipation* at the same time. One of his assistants, William Lloyd Garrison, thought the Quaker approach was too slow and pushed for the immediate freeing of slaves. In 1831, he started *The Liberator,* warning, "I will be as harsh as truth and as uncompromising as justice." After stories spread that Nat Turner had been inspired to revolt because he had read the newspaper, Garrison got much more attention. Elijah Lovejoy, abolitionist editor of the *Alton Observer* in Illinois, was murdered by a mob in 1837.

In the 1830s, abolitionists began writing thousands of letters to Congress pushing it to act against slavery. Congress worried about these enough that the House passed the Gag Rule in 1836, which said that any protest against slavery would be tabled without discussion (in other words, totally ignored). When the postmaster general ordered that abolitionist material addressed to the South could be destroyed by postal officials, Congress did not criticize the ruling.

RESULTS: Congress ignored abolitionist petitions, and the abolitionists used this as an example of how undemocratic methods were used by the South to silence criticism. Rather than hurt the abolitionists, Congress's methods actually gained sympathy for them. In 1844, the Gag Rule was finally defeated.

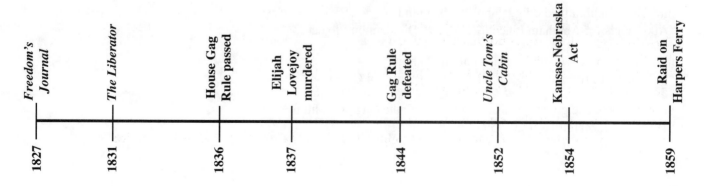

Freedom's Journal	*The Liberator*	House Gag Rule passed	Elijah Lovejoy murdered	Gag Rule defeated	*Uncle Tom's Cabin*	Kansas-Nebraska Act	Raid on Harpers Ferry
1827	1831	1836	1837	1844	1852	1854	1859

Name: _____ Date: _____

Abolitionists Act, Congress Reacts: Reinforcement

Directions: Complete the following activities, essays, and challenges on your own paper.

ACTIVITIES:

1. Discuss the effect of letter-writing campaigns. What makes them work? Why do many of them fail?
2. Discuss efforts that are often made today through protests and demonstrations. Do you admire these people? Why or why not?

ESSAYS:

1. As an abolitionist, how would you react to the Gag Rule?
2. As Amos Kendall, the postmaster general, how would you justify telling postmasters to destroy those abolitionist materials?
3. What kinds of issues were raised by the Gag Rule?

CHALLENGES:

1. What was Horace Mann's great interest? How successful was he in reaching his goals?
2. What made Elizabeth Blackwell important?
3. Why was *Freedom's Journal* unusual?
4. What newspaper did Benjamin Lundy publish? Why did Garrison leave it?
5. What gave added prestige to *The Liberator* among anti-slavery people?
6. What happened to Elijah Lovejoy that made him a hero to abolitionists?
7. Why didn't the South appreciate all the letters Congress was receiving from the North?
8. How did the Gag Rule try to discourage abolitionists from writing petitions to Congress?
9. What did post offices do with abolitionist materials sent to the South?
10. When was the Gag Rule finally repealed?

NATIONAL STANDARDS CORRELATIONS:

NCSS Ve: (Individuals, Groups, & Institutions) Identify and describe examples of tensions between belief systems and government policies and laws.
NSH Era 4, Standard 3: The extension, restrictions, and reorganization of political democracy after 1800

WEBSITES:

http://www.archives.gov/exhibits/treasures_of_congress/text/page10_text.html
"Struggles over Slavery: The 'Gag' Rule," The U.S. National Archives and Records Administration

http://lincoln.lib.niu.edu/digitalabolitionism.html
"Abolitionism," Abraham Lincoln Historical Digitization Project

http://www.loc.gov/exhibits/african/afam006.html
"Influence of Prominent Abolitionists," The Library of Congress

http://www.senate.gov/artandhistory/history/minute/Gag_Rule.htm
"1801–1850: March 16, 1836, Gag Rule," U.S. Senate

Nicholas Trist Makes Peace With Mexico

James K. Polk

As Nicholas Trist, chief clerk of the State Department, sat across from Mexican diplomats at Guadalupe-Hidalgo, he held the fate of California and New Mexico in his hands. He might have felt more important except he knew he was not supposed to be at that table on that day.

The United States and Mexico had been neighbors but not friends since Mexico had gained independence from Spain. Troubles began with arguments between officials and Santa Fe traders, the Texas Revolution, and disputes over Native-American attacks and unpaid bills. Some Americans in California accepted Mexican rule without protest, but others wanted the United States to own it. In 1846, the Bear Flag Revolt broke out in California; when news reached the Americans involved, they flew the stars and stripes.

Fighting had begun before war was declared. General Zachary Taylor had crossed the Nueces River, and one of his patrols was attacked. President Polk asked Congress for war, charging that "American blood has been shed on American soil." Most Americans supported the war at first, but Abraham Lincoln and John C. Calhoun both saw the war as a way to seize land.

During the Mexican War (1846–1848), American troops attacked on several fronts. Taylor's army advanced into the region south of the Rio Grande. General Stephen Kearny's army captured Santa Fe and moved across the deserts and mountains into California. General Winfield Scott led an invasion of Mexico, attacking Vera Cruz on the coast. Trist traveled with Scott's army as an agent of the State Department. Trist was told that he could offer as much as $20 million for California and New Mexico and $5 million more for Lower California.

Trist always tried to do his duty, but he found that traveling with Scott was very difficult. Scott did not like him because he thought Trist was a spy sent by the president to report any failure. After Trist became ill, Scott felt sorry for him and sent him a jar of jelly. After that, a much better relationship existed between them. Trist was also finding it difficult to make peace with Mexico since its government was falling apart. In late 1847, he found a group willing to make peace.

Then Trist received orders to return home, but he did not know which way to go. If he returned, the war might go on endlessly. If he stayed, he defied a specific order from the president. He asked Scott what he should do, and Scott asked him to stay. He ignored the order and made peace with Mexico. The treaty said that the United States would receive California and New Mexico in return for $15 million, and it established the Texas boundary at the Rio Grande. President Polk was angry with Trist for defying orders, but he saw the need to end the war quickly, and the terms of the treaty were good.

RESULTS: The Senate approved the treaty in February 1848, and the war was over. The United States had gained 529,000 square miles of valuable land and had new outlets for trade with Asia. Polk got even with Trist for disobeying orders by refusing to pay his salary and expenses. It was not until after Trist died that Congress paid these bills in 1871.

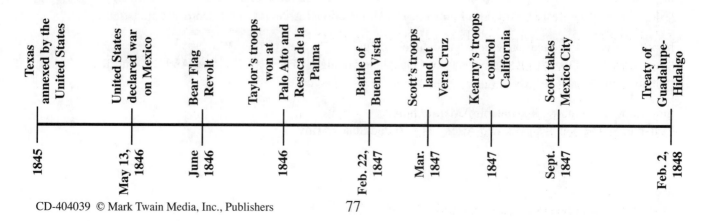

Texas annexed by the United States	United States declared war on Mexico	Bear Flag Revolt	Taylor's troops won at Palo Alto and Resaca de la Palma	Battle of Buena Vista	Scott's troops land at Vera Cruz	Kearny's troops control California	Scott takes Mexico City	Treaty of Guadalupe-Hidalgo
1845	May 13, 1846	June 1846	1846	Feb. 22, 1847	Mar. 1847	1847	Sept. 1847	Feb. 2, 1848

Name: _____ Date: _____

Nicholas Trist Makes Peace With Mexico: Reinforcement

Directions: Complete the following activities, essays, and challenges on your own paper.

ACTIVITIES:

1. The United States has never been proud of the Mexican War. Discuss why some wars make nations proud and others become embarrassments.
2. Locate a map of the war, and point out the major military movement. Looking at the topography of the region, point out the problems Kearny faced on his expedition.

ESSAYS:

1. Violating a president's orders is risky. If you were Trist, what would you have done? Why?
2. Looking at a map showing the Mexican Cession, would you say it was a better or worse deal than the Louisiana Purchase? Why?
3. Do you think Polk and later presidents were fair to Trist? Why?

CHALLENGES:

1. What were some problems between the United States and Mexico?
2. What was California's revolution against Mexico called?
3. What phrase in Polk's message to Congress stirred up support for war?
4. Who were two early critics of war?
5. Looking at maps of the war, which American general was at Monterrey?
    At Los Angeles?
    At Mexico City?
6. Why was Trist with Scott's army? Why did Scott think he was there?
    Why did Polk's order to return arrive at a bad time for Trist?
7. How much did the United States pay for California and New Mexico?
9. How did Polk feel about Trist? Why?
10. How did Polk get even with Trist?

NAT_ \)NAL STANDARDS CORRELATIONS:

NCSS _f: (Civic Ideals & Practices) Identify and explain the roles of formal and informal political actors in influencing and shaping public policy and decision-making.
NSH Era 4, Standard 1: United States territorial expansion between 1801 and 1861, and how it affected relations with external powers and Native Americans

WEBSITES:

http://www.archives.gov/publications/prologue/2005/summer/mexico-1.html
"Monuments, Manifest Destiny, and Mexico," The U.S. National Archives and Records Administration

http://archives.gov/education/lessons/guadalupe-hidalgo/
"Teaching With Documents: The Treaty of Guadalupe-Hidalgo," The U.S. National Archives and Records Administration

http://army.mil/cmh-pg/books/amh/AMH-08.htm
"Chapter 8: The Mexican War and After," The United States Army

Sutter's Secret Is Told—A Gold Rush Follows

Johann Sutter

If one reads early American writings about California, one finds it portrayed as a paradise in the hands of a lazy people. Mexican settlements in California were few: missions, ranches, and a few towns. The climate and soil made life easy for the settler, and the Native Americans provided a cheap source of labor. A few Americans went to California before 1840: fur trappers, whalers, and cattle buyers. A few arrived overland, but most came by sea around South America. Some settled; others, like Jedediah Smith, the mountain man, were just passing through.

Among the American settlers were Thomas Larkin, a leading merchant at Monterrey; John Marsh, who owned a big ranch; and Johann Sutter, who settled in northern California. Sutter was originally Swiss but had come to the United States in 1834 to avoid paying his debts. Five years later, he was in California, became a Mexican citizen, and borrowed money to buy land. When large numbers of Americans began coming overland to California, many stayed at Sutter's ranch while they rested after their long trip. He was a good host, but many took advantage of him.

The overland trip was a difficult experience. The first settlers to try it, the Bidwell party, looked like scarecrows when they arrived in 1841. The next year, Lansford Hastings wrote a book, *The Emigrant's Guide to California*, giving suggestions on overland travel to would-be settlers. Not everything in the book had been checked out, and it included an unexplored shortcut that became known as the Hastings Cutoff. The Donner party tried the Hastings Cutoff in 1846, got trapped in a snowstorm in the Sierra Nevadas, and some survived by eating the flesh of those who died.

When the Bear Flag Revolt broke out, there were about 700 Americans in California; when they learned of the Mexican War, they quickly switched from a bear flag to the American flag. After the war, California became American territory with a large Mexican-American population. The mix might have stayed that way if a discovery had not taken place on Sutter's property. Sutter had sent a group of men to build a sawmill on the American River and had put James Marshall in charge of the project. While walking down the stream bed on January 24, 1848, he noticed something shiny in the water. It looked like gold. He put it in a sack and took it to Sutter. They tried to keep it a secret, but word leaked; in May the gold rush began.

It took time for word to reach the East, but when President Polk included reports of the gold find in California in a message to Congress, it became official. In 1849, thousands of men kissed their wives and children goodbye and headed for California. There were three basic ways to go: around South America, across Panama (then by ship to California), or across the continent by land. The most commonly taken route was overland.

RESULTS: Men who had dreams of quick riches were usually disappointed. Prices in California were very high, and chances of finding the "big bonanza" were few; but that did not keep them from coming. Living in nearly all-male camps, working in ice-cold water, and sheltered by a tent or lean-to, some dreamed of home. Others thought only of the mansion and servants they would have when luck shined on them.

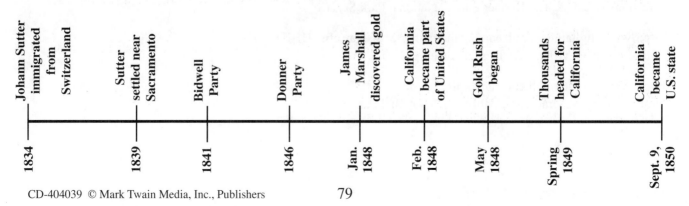

Johann Sutter immigrated from Switzerland	Sutter settled near Sacramento	Bidwell Party	Donner Party	James Marshall discovered gold	California became part of United States	Gold Rush began	Thousands headed for California	California became U.S. state
1834	1839	1841	1846	Jan. 1848	Feb. 1848	May 1848	Spring 1849	Sept. 9, 1850

Name: _____ Date: _____

Sutter's Secret Is Told—A Gold Rush Follows: Reinforcement

Directions: Complete the following activities, essays, and challenges on your own paper.

ACTIVITIES:

1. When gold was found, the men formed mining districts and wrote rules. Have the class write rules for a mining camp.
2. Have the class discuss what motivates people to try to get rich quick, even when odds are more in favor of failure. What modern parallels are there to a gold rush mentality?

ESSAYS:

1. After reading about the Donner party's experience, do you think the gold rush would have been enough to encourage you to travel to California? Why?
2. Examine a map of the western United States and discuss problems the overlanders would have faced.
3. How do you think people lived in gold camps: food, shelter, work, rules, etc.?

CHALLENGES:

1. Who were the first Americans to go to California?
2. Why did Johann Sutter leave Switzerland and come to America?
3. Why was Sutter's ranch important for settlers arriving in California?
4. What was important about the Bidwell party?
5. Why was following the Hastings Cutoff dangerous for travelers?
6. What happened to the Donner party?
7. Who discovered gold in January 1848?
8. What routes did people take to California?
9. Which of these routes was the most commonly taken?
10. Even if a man found gold in California, why was it hard for him to get rich?

NATIONAL STANDARDS CORRELATIONS:

NCSS IIIi: (People, Places, & Environments) Describe ways that historical events have been influenced by, and have influenced, physical and human geographic factors in local, regional, national, and global settings.

NSH Era 4, Standard 2: How the industrial revolution, increasing immigration, the rapid expansion of slavery, and the westward movement changed the lives of Americans and led toward regional tensions

WEBSITES:

http://memory.loc.gov/ammem/cbhtml/cbgold.html
"The Discovery of Gold," The Library of Congress

http://www.nps.gov/cali/cali/history3.htm
"Hastings Cutoff & The Donner Party," National Park Service

http://www.digitalhistory.uh.edu/database/article_display.cfm?HHID=303
"The Donner Party Period," Digital History

http://www.nps.gov/cali/cali/site10.htm
"Sutter's Fort—Sacramento, California," National Park Service

Daniel Webster Delivers the Seventh of March Speech

Daniel Webster

Daniel Webster was the most noted orator (public speaker) of his time, and whenever he debated, large crowds gathered. When he announced that he would speak on the controversial Compromise of 1850, the nation waited with great interest. Many senators had spoken already—Henry Clay and Stephen Douglas for it, John C. Calhoun against it.

The importance of a speech by Webster would have amazed his early teachers. In school he was good at everything, except public speaking. After graduating from college, he became one of the best-known lawyers in the nation and argued important cases before the Supreme Court. After five years in the House, he became a senator from Massachusetts in 1827. There he had given a dramatic speech against the nullifiers, in which he proclaimed, "Liberty and Union, now and forever, one and inseparable!" While he agreed with Andrew Jackson on the need to keep the Union together, they disagreed strongly on most other issues. He joined with Clay in forming the Whig party. In 1841, Webster became secretary of state, but in 1844, he returned to the Senate.

Webster was not enthusiastic about the Mexican War; he thought Polk should have worked harder on a diplomatic solution. In 1846, the Wilmot Proviso was debated. It forbade slavery in any territory taken from Mexico. Webster supported it because he opposed slavery on moral grounds. The Proviso passed in the House but was defeated because of southern opposition in the Senate.

With the end of the war and the election of Zachary Taylor as president, the slavery issue was much on Webster's mind. California's gold rush had increased its population enough for it to became a state. To admit California would break the even balance of free and slave states. Other issues were also on people's minds as well. Northern states were passing personal liberty laws making it difficult for slaveowners to recapture runaway slaves. Abolitionists opposed the slave trade in the District of Columbia. Texas was in deep debt. The settlers in New Mexico and Utah needed organized government.

Henry Clay put these issues together in one bill and enlisted help from Senator Stephen Douglas. Known as the Compromise of 1850, it would: (1) admit California as a free state, (2) organize New Mexico and Utah territories and let the people decide whether to be slave or free, (3) tighten the fugitive slave law, (4) end slave trade in the District of Columbia, and (5) give Texas $10,000,000 in exchange for land in west Texas, which would become part of New Mexico.

RESULTS: On March 7, Webster stood and said, "I wish to speak today ... as an American ... I speak today for the preservation of the Union. Hear me for my cause." For three hours, he spoke of the tensions pulling the nation apart. He said that instead of talking about secession (leaving the Union), Americans should enjoy the "fresh air of liberty and union." His speech helped make compromise possible, but the time for compromises was coming to a close.

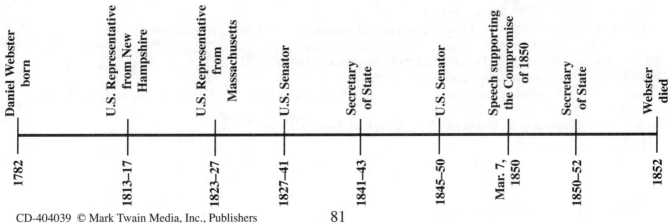

Daniel Webster born	U.S. Representative from New Hampshire	U.S. Representative from Massachusetts	U.S. Senator	Secretary of State	U.S. Senator	Speech supporting the Compromise of 1850	Secretary of State	Webster died
1782	1813–17	1823–27	1827–41	1841–43	1845–50	Mar. 7, 1850	1850–52	1852

Name: _____ Date: _____

Daniel Webster Delivers the Seventh
of March Speech: Reinforcement

Directions: Complete the following activities, essays, and challenges on your own paper.

ACTIVITIES:

1. Have the class examine a map to see how much of the nation was affected by the Compromise of 1850.
2. Have the class debate the issues by dividing the class into groups of northern, southern, and border-state senators.

ESSAYS:

1. What makes compromises possible? Do you think they are always good?
2. As a southerner in Congress, what parts of the Compromise of 1850 would you have supported? Why?
3. As a northerner in Congress, what parts of the Compromise of 1850 would you have supported? Why?

CHALLENGES:

1. What was Daniel Webster's weakest subject as a student?
2. What had been the occasion for the "Liberty and Union" statement?
3. What position did Webster take on the Wilmot Proviso?
4. As a southern slaveowner, how would you have felt about personal liberty laws?
5. What was the theme of the Seventh of March speech?
6. How was California affected by the Compromise of 1850?
7. How was New Mexico affected by the Compromise of 1850?
8. How was Texas affected by the Compromise of 1850?
9. How was slavery in the District of Columbia affected by the Compromise of 1850?
10. How were fugitive slaves affected by the Compromise of 1850?

NATIONAL STANDARDS CORRELATIONS:

NCSS Xf: (Civic Ideals & Practices) Identify and explain the roles of formal and informal political actors in influencing and shaping public policy and decision-making.
NSH Era 5, Standard 1: The causes of the Civil War

WEBSITES:

http://memory.loc.gov/cgi-bin/query/r?ammem/mcc:@field%28DOCID+@lit%28mcc/091%29$29
"Daniel Webster's notes for his speech to the United States Senate favoring the Compromise of 1850, 7 March 1850," The Library of Congress

http://www.senate.gov/artandhistory/history/common/generic/Featured_Bio_Webster.htm
"Daniel Webster: A Featured Biography," United States Senate

http://memory.loc.gov/ammem/ndlpedu/collections/slavery/history.html
"From Slavery to Freedom: The African-American Pamphlet Collection, 1822–1909," The Library of Congress

http://www.digitalhistory.uh.edu/database/article_display.cfm?HHID=321
"The Political Crisis of the 1840s," Digital History

Uncle Tom's Cabin **Is Published**

Harriet Beecher Stowe

Readers laughed at Topsy's humor, trembled as Eliza escaped, and wept when Uncle Tom died. These people were imaginary, but to readers, they were real. For the first time, many began to see slaves as real people suffering terrible injustices. No novel had ever stirred such a response. The success of *Uncle Tom's Cabin* exceeded any ambition of its author, Harriet Beecher Stowe, and its effect stirred world opinion.

Mrs. Stowe came from a family of famous ministers. Her father, Lyman Beecher, was a man of strong opinions. Her favorite brother, Henry Ward Beecher, became the most famous minister in the country. She married Calvin Stowe, a minister and professor at Lane Theological Seminary in Cincinnati where her father was president. To add to her husband's small salary, she wrote short stories whenever she could. However, with seven children, she was very busy.

The family often discussed slavery. To them, it was a social sin and not an individual sin. The slaveowner was caught in an evil system but might be a fine person. This view was confirmed by a visit to a Kentucky plantation where the master was kind to the slaves, but they were still property bought and sold. She met runaway slaves, and they told her about the terrible conditions they escaped. Thoughts of slavery tormented her.

In 1850, she and her husband moved to Maine where Professor Stowe taught at Bowdoin College. While visiting with her brother Edward, they talked about the Compromise of 1850, which both opposed. Her sister-in-law wrote Harriet, "If I could just use the pen as you can, I would write something that would make this whole nation feel what an accursed thing slavery is." Mrs. Stowe answered that she could do little writing because of the baby, "But I will do it at last. I will write the thing if I live."

As she sat in church one gloomy Sunday, images crossed her mind. She saw a black man being whipped, and the dying man asking God's forgiveness for those who had beaten him. She thought of escaped slaves she had met in Cincinnati and their stories. She rushed home and began to write, and when she ran out of writing paper, she wrote on a grocery sack. After writing the end of the book, she developed the other characters.

Except for Simon Legree, the whites in the book were not evil. The Shelbys, who first owned Tom, were kind, and Mrs. Shelby described slavery as "a curse to the master and a curse to the slave." St. Clare, Tom's second owner, wondered about the wisdom of beating slaves. Simon Legree, the villain of the story, was a New Englander who rejected his mother's love to live a drunken and evil life. Together with his two African-American henchmen, they made life miserable for the slaves. Uncle Tom's Christian behavior was too much for Legree, and after Tom refused to pick up a whip and beat a woman slave, he was killed by Legree's allies, Quimbo and Sambo. As Tom lay dying, the Shelbys' son came and took him home.

The story was published first in the *National Era*, then in book form.

RESULTS: The book was an instant bestseller. It sold 300,000 copies in its first year in the United States and 1.5 million copies later in England.

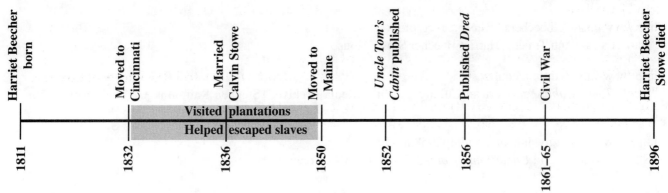

Name: _____ Date: _____

Uncle Tom's Cabin Is Published: Reinforcement

Directions: Complete the following activities, essays, and challenges on your own paper.

ACTIVITIES:

1. Have students discuss books they have read that have affected the way they look at life.
2. Ask students how they would react to sudden fame like Mrs. Stowe received. (You might tell them that she was very shy and much preferred reading to being the center of attention.)

ESSAYS:

1. A novel is a story about people who do not exist. How can a novel be used to inform people about a controversial issue?
2. The South was very angry over *Uncle Tom's Cabin*, which surprised Mrs. Stowe. Why do you think this surprised her?
3. As an abolitionist, how would you have reacted to the characters in the story and the successful sales of the book? Why?

CHALLENGES:

1. Who were two well-known ministers in Harriet Stowe's family?
2. What did Calvin Stowe do for a living?
3. How did Harriet add to the family income?
4. How much firsthand knowledge did she have about slavery?
5. Would she have agreed with abolitionists who said slaveowners were terrible people who should suffer for their crimes? Why?
6. Who inspired her to write a book about slavery?
7. What part of *Uncle Tom's Cabin* did she write first?
8. Name two slaves mentioned in the book besides Uncle Tom.
9. When a boss is referred to today as a "Simon Legree," what does the speaker mean?
10. How many copies of *Uncle Tom's Cabin* did the English buy?

NATIONAL STANDARDS CORRELATIONS:

NCSS Ic: (Culture) Explain and give examples of how language, literature, the arts, architecture, other artifacts, traditions, beliefs, values, and behaviors contribute to the development and transmission of culture.
NSH Era 4, Standard 4: The sources and character of cultural, religious, and social reform movements in the antebellum period

WEBSITES:

http://www.harrietbeecherstowecenter.org/life/
"Harriet's Life and Times," Harriet Beecher Stowe House

http://www.iath.virginia/edu/utc/
"*Uncle Tom's Cabin* & American Culture: A Multi-Media Archive," Stephen Railton & the University of Virginia

http://www.pbs.org/wgbh/aia/part4/4p2958.html
"Slave Narratives and *Uncle Tom's Cabin*," The Library of Congress

The Nation Focuses on "Bleeding Kansas"

Stephen Douglas

If a stranger had told you in 1853, that the newspapers would be full of news about Shawnee Mission, Topeka, Lawrence, and Pottawatomie Creek in the next three years, you would have thought he was insane. History is full of such twists of fate, and the impossible becomes reality.

The reason for Kansas becoming headline news goes back to the rapid growth of California and interest in building a railroad across the continent. A survey had already been run for a railroad from New Orleans to the West Coast, and the Gadsden Purchase made it possible to build that railroad south of the Gila River. Many thought there would be only one railroad, so northern states much preferred a more northern route. As a senator from Illinois, it was logical to Stephen Douglas that it be built west from Chicago. A railroad requires customers in order to be profitable; however, settlers will not move onto land that has not been surveyed and where there is no government to protect life or property.

Douglas proposed the Kansas-Nebraska Bill in 1854. It provided that Kansas and Nebraska territories be formed and allowed the people who settled there to decide whether or not there would be slavery. This idea was called popular sovereignty. He knew there would be opposition because it would overturn the long-standing Missouri Compromise, which had blocked any slavery north of 36°30'. Kansas and Nebraska were above that line. Southerners and President Franklin Pierce backed it; many northerners were opposed. The bill barely passed.

People on both sides realized it was important that their group get control in Kansas. Lying west of Missouri, it might threaten slavery in that state, so Missouri Senator David Atchison urged southerners to settle there. Many northerners also saw the importance, and the New England Emigrant Aid Company was formed to help New Englanders to settle there. Reverend Henry Ward Beecher said that rifles rather than Bibles would determine the issue, and boxes of "Beecher's Bibles" (rifles) were sent to Kansas.

Andrew Reeder was appointed territorial governor. When he called an election, nearly 5,000 Missourians crossed into Kansas and voted. Their vote was enough to win the election, and a pro-slave legislature was set up at Lecompton. The anti-slavery people ignored it and set up their own legislature at Topeka.

Acts of violence often took place. A pro-slave posse attacked the anti-slavery community of Lawrence, threw its printing press into the river, and tore up the town. John Brown, an abolitionist, led a group of men to Pottawatomie Creek, a pro-slave town, and killed five men and boys, then split their skulls with a sword. North and South, Republicans and Democrats watched happenings in Kansas with horror, and each blamed the other for the violence.

RESULTS: Kansas remained tense for years after this, and during the Civil War, trouble often broke out between Missourians and Kansans. In 1861, Kansas became a state.

Directions: Complete the following activities, essays, and challenges on your own paper.

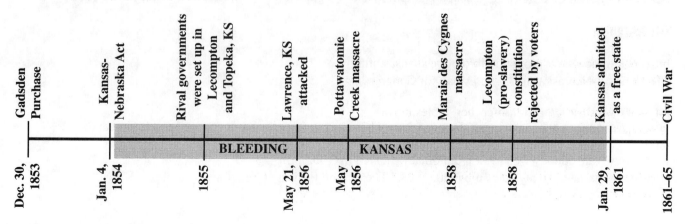

Gadsden Purchase	Kansas-Nebraska Act	Rival governments were set up in Lecompton and Topeka, KS	Lawrence, KS attacked	Pottawatomie Creek massacre	Marais des Cygnes massacre	Lecompton (pro-slavery) constitution rejected by voters	Kansas admitted as a free state	Civil War
		BLEEDING		KANSAS				
Dec. 30, 1853	Jan. 4, 1854	1855	May 21, 1856	May 1856	1858	1858	Jan. 29, 1861	1861–65

Name: _____ Date: _____

The Nation Focuses on "Bleeding Kansas": Reinforcement

ACTIVITIES:

1. Discuss how issues often flare up in unexpected places that can affect national affairs.
2. Examine a map of Kansas and locate key sites where trouble occurred. Why were they all in eastern Kansas?

ESSAYS:

1. As one of these people, how would you feel about the Kansas-Nebraska bill? Why?
    A. A person wanting cheap land for yourself
    B. A southerner
    C. An abolitionist
2. With all the trouble in Kansas, why would a person want to move there?
3. Many motives have been given for Douglas's decision. Which of the following seem logical to you?
    A. He wanted to be president.
    B. He did not think there would ever be slavery in Kansas anyway.
    C. He believed that the people should have a right to decide issues for themselves.

CHALLENGES:

1. What was the reason for the Gadsden Purchase?
2. Where did Stephen Douglas want a railroad to the Pacific to start? Why?
3. How would forming Kansas and Nebraska make a railroad across the Plains possible?
4. What previous law did the Kansas-Nebraska bill overturn? How?
5. What was a "Beecher's Bible"?
6. Who was president when the Kansas-Nebraska bill was discussed? How did he feel about it?
7. What happened when Governor Reeder called for elections?
8. How did John Brown add to the tension in Kansas?
9. Who did Republicans in the North blame for the trouble in Kansas?
10. When did Kansas become a state?

NATIONAL STANDARDS CORRELATIONS:

NCSS VIc: (Power, Authority, & Governance) Analyze and explain ideas and governmental mechanisms to meet needs and wants of citizens, regulate territory, manage conflict, and establish order and security.
NSH Ear 4, Standard 3: The extension, restriction, and reorganization of political democracy after 1800

WEBSITES:

http://www.loc.gov/rr/program/bib/ourdocs/kansas.html
"The Kansas-Nebraska Act," The Library of Congress

http://www.kshs.org/portraits/beecher_bibles.htm
"Beecher Bibles: A Kansas Portrait," Kansas State Historical Society

http://www.yale.edu/lawweb/avalon/diplomacy/mexico/mx1853.htm
"Gadsden Purchase Treaty: December 30, 1853," The Avalon Project at Yale Law School

Buchanan Is Elected in 1856

James Buchanan

The issue of Kansas caused hard feelings between the North and South. In 1856, Senator Charles Sumner of Massachusetts attacked the Kansas-Nebraska bill in the "Crime Against Kansas" speech. He named people he thought were responsible for "Bleeding Kansas," including Senator Stephen Douglas (Illinois) and Andrew Butler (South Carolina). Douglas tried to ignore this personal attack but commented that Sumner was going to provoke some fool to assault him, and that was exactly what happened. Senator Butler had a nephew, Preston Brooks, in the House. Brooks walked into the Senate chamber and beat Sumner with a cane until he slumped to the floor in a pool of blood. An effort was made to expel Brooks from the House, but it failed to get the two-thirds needed. Brooks resigned but was reelected by a nearly unanimous vote. Canes were sent from all over the South to replace the one he had broken on Sumner's head. The attack occurred just before the Democrats met to choose their presidential candidate for 1856.

Because of the Kansas problem, the Democratic convention ignored Pierce and Douglas to find a less controversial candidate. The man chosen was James Buchanan, a 65-year-old Pennsylvanian, who had been a lawyer, a member of both Houses of Congress, a diplomat, and a former secretary of state. He did not consider slavery moral, but he felt the federal government could do nothing about it in the states. He had supported the refusal to send abolitionist material in the mail and had opposed the Wilmot Proviso. He had many friends in the South.

Northern and southern Whigs had split over Kansas-Nebraska; some in the North joined the Republicans, and others joined the Know-Nothings. In the South, Whigs either became Know-Nothings or Democrats. The Know-Nothings were white, native-born Americans who had formed the Supreme Order of the Star-Spangled Banner (SSSB). They feared the increasing number of Catholics and immigrants and wanted to keep them from ever holding office. If asked about the SSSB, they were to say, "I know nothing about it."

The Republican party was formed by former Whigs, unhappy Democrats, and reformers. Among those joining were senators like William Seward (New York), Salmon Chase (Ohio), and Charles Sumner (Massachusetts). An attorney from Springfield, Illinois—Abraham Lincoln—also joined. Many at the 1856 Republican convention realized they had little chance of winning and gave the nomination to John C. Frémont, hero of Western exploration. Since Frémont was wealthy, he could pay for his campaign out of his own pocket.

RESULTS: In the North, the campaign was between Democrats and Republicans; in the South, it was between Democrats and the American party. Democrats warned that a Frémont election would drive the South out of the Union. Republicans chanted back, "Free Soil, Free Speech, Free Men, Frémont." There was great enthusiasm on all sides, but when the electoral votes were counted, Buchanan won. There were times, however, when he wished that he *had* lost.

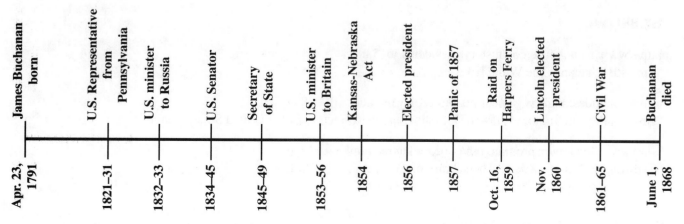

James Buchanan born	U.S. Representative from Pennsylvania	U.S. minister to Russia	U.S. Senator	Secretary of State	U.S. minister to Britain	Kansas-Nebraska Act	Elected president	Panic of 1857	Raid on Harpers Ferry	Lincoln elected president	Civil War	Buchanan died
Apr. 23, 1791	1821–31	1832–33	1834–45	1845–49	1853–56	1854	1856	1857	Oct. 16, 1859	Nov. 1860	1861–65	June 1, 1868

Name: _____ Date: _____

Buchanan Is Elected in 1856: Reinforcement

Directions: Complete the following activities, essays, and challenges on your own paper.

ACTIVITIES:

1. Immigration from Ireland and Germany had been heavy in the 1840s. Have students research to find out from where immigrants come today and how people react to them.
2. Ask what students think would have happened if Frémont had been elected. Do they think the Civil War might have come four years earlier? Why?

ESSAYS:

1. What were some of the big issues of 1856? How would you have felt about them? Why?
2. Do you feel that Buchanan was chosen because of his record or because of his lack of a strong position against slavery? Why?
3. In the election, Buchanan got 45 percent of the popular vote but won in the Electoral College. As a Republican of that time, would you have felt bad about losing, or would you have seen the election as a sign of future success?

CHALLENGES:

1. Who gave the "Crime Against Kansas" speech? Why was it unpopular with Preston Brooks?
2. Why did people send canes to Preston Brooks?
3. Why did Democrats pass over Pierce and Douglas when looking for a candidate?
4. How did Buchanan feel about slavery?
5. Where did former Whigs go in 1856?
6. For what did the acronym "SSSB" stand?
7. From where did the name "Know Nothing" come?
8. Who did the Know-Nothings want to keep out of office?
9. Why did Seward and other important Republicans choose not to run in 1856?
10. What slogan was popular among Republicans that year?

NATIONAL STANDARDS CORRELATIONS:

NCSS Xf: (Civic Ideals & Practices) Identify and explain the roles of formal and informal political actors in influencing and shaping public policy and decision-making.
NSH Era 4, Standard 3: The extension, restriction, and reorganization of political democracy after 1800

WEBSITES:

http://www.whitehouse.gov/history/presidents/jb15.html
"James Buchanan," The White House

http://bioguide.congress.gov/scripts/biodisplay.pl?index=B000885
"Brooks, Preston Smith, (1819–1857)," Biographical Directory of the United States Congress

http://www.loc.gov/rr/program/bib/ourdocs/kansas.html
"The Kansas-Nebraska Act," The Library of Congress

John Brown Attacks Harpers Ferry

As John Brown watched the proceedings at his trial, even his friends were making him angry. They tried to defend him by saying he was insane. People had said the same thing about his mother, his aunt, his first wife, and some of his sons. It was the world that was insane, talking about slavery as if it were some legal point, or saying it was a good system or an issue with two sides. To John Brown, the fate of the African-American slave was a cause worth dying for. He often quoted the scripture: "Without the shedding of blood, there is no forgiveness of sin."

Slavery was a technical point of law to some. Chief Justice Roger Taney in the *Dred Scott* decision (1857) denied that Congress had any power to keep slavery out of the territories and described African-Americans as an "inferior order." That same year, George Fitzhugh wrote in *Cannibals All:* "What a glorious thing to man is slavery." Hinton Helper, also a southerner, wrote *The Impending Crisis of the South*, which attacked slavery, not because it was evil for the slaves, but because it hurt the poor whites. Debates in Congress, in courts, and in books were mere words. John Brown was not a man of words, but action.

In Kansas, he led the attack on Pottawatomie Creek. After that, he traveled to Boston and talked with abolitionists. Then he returned to Kansas and used it as a base to steal slaves and horses in Missouri. In one raid, he killed a farmer who got in his way. However, a direct blow on slavery was what he really desired. He persuaded the Boston abolitionists (the Secret Six) to give him $10,000 for his venture, and he planned his attack on the small, quiet town of Harpers Ferry, Virginia.

Located on the Potomac River, Harpers Ferry had a federal arsenal, armory, and rifle works; it was also in a slave state. His plan was to arm local slaves, which would signal a general slave rebellion. He and his new army could stay up in the mountains and fight off enemies until victory was won and the last slave was freed. He tried to persuade free African-Americans in the North to join him, but they thought the plan was too risky.

On October 16, 1859, Brown's men attacked Harpers Ferry, cut telegraph lines, and stopped the morning train. Men were sent out to bring in slaves from nearby farms and to gather a few white hostages. A free African-American who worked for the railroad tried to run away, but he was shot in the back. Brown then allowed the train to leave, and the engineer sent a message that Harpers Ferry was under attack. Colonel Robert E. Lee was sent to Harpers Ferry with some marines. By the time they arrived, Brown's men were in the engine house. After Brown turned down an offer to surrender, the marines attacked and captured the raiders.

RESULTS: Brown was tried and found guilty of treason against the state of Virginia. He told the court, "If it is deemed necessary that I should forfeit my life ... let it be done." He became a symbol of self-sacrifice, and as Union soldiers marched, they sang, "John Brown's body lies a-moldering in the grave, as we go marching on."

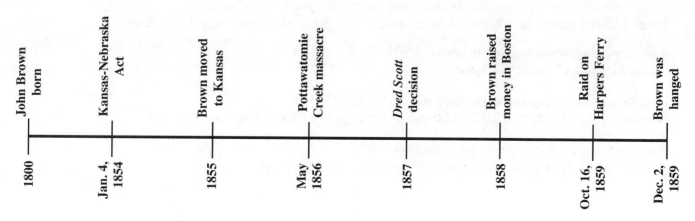

John Brown born — 1800

Kansas-Nebraska Act — Jan. 4, 1854

Brown moved to Kansas — 1855

Pottawatomie Creek massacre — May 1856

Dred Scott decision — 1857

Brown raised money in Boston — 1858

Raid on Harpers Ferry — Oct. 16, 1859

Brown was hanged — Dec. 2, 1859

Name: _____ Date: _____

John Brown Attacks Harpers Ferry: Reinforcement

Directions: Complete the following activities, essays, and challenges on your own paper.

ACTIVITIES:

1. Compare Brown to Don Quixote as a person who wanted to make the world right and sacrificed everything for "an impossible dream."
2. Discuss whether or not the class thinks the Secret Six were responsible for the attack on Harpers Ferry.

ESSAYS:

1. The South became very frightened by the raid on Harpers Ferry. Why?
2. Do you think of Brown as insane or as a hero? Why?
3. For the plan to work, what was needed? Do you think it ever had a chance of success? Why or why not?

CHALLENGES:

1. As an abolitionist, how would you feel about the *Dred Scott* decision?
2. As an abolitionist, how would you feel about George Fitzhugh?
3. As an abolitionist, how would you feel about the concerns of Hinton Helper?
4. Who were the Secret Six? How did they help Brown?
5. Why did Brown attack Harpers Ferry?
6. How would capturing Harpers Ferry help his plan?
7. If you were a free African-American, why might you not want to join Brown's army?
8. Why did Brown allow the train to leave? Why was that a mistake?
9. Who led the marines against Brown?
10. How did Brown feel about his execution?

NATIONAL STANDARDS CORRELATIONS:

NCSS Xf: (Civic Ideals & Practices) Identify and explain the roles of formal and informal political actors in influencing and shaping public policy and decision-making.

NSH Era 4, Standard 4: The sources and character of cultural, religious, and social reform movements in the antebellum period

WEBSITES:

http://www.yale.edu/lawweb/avalon/treatise/john_brown/john_brown.htm
"Life, Trial and Execution of Captain John Brown; 1859," The Avalon Project at Yale Law School

http://www.yale.edu/glc/archive/1057.htm
"George Fitzhugh," The Gilder Lehrman Center

http://usinfo.state.gov/usa/infousa/facts/democrac/21.htm
"Introduction to the Court Opinion on the Dred Scott Case," U.S. Department of State

http://www.pbs.org/wgbh/aia/part4/4p1550.html
"People & Events: John Brown 1800–1859," Public Broadcasting Service

South Carolina Secedes

Across the nation, people gathered at newspaper offices and at the telegraphers in the railroad stations in November 1860. As returns came in, the news was joyous for some, disturbing for some, and grim for others. The reason for all this excitement was the presidential election that had just taken place—one that would have more effect on the future of the nation than any before.

The election process had begun in April with a wild Democratic convention in Charleston, South Carolina, but it produced no harmony and no candidate. Some southern delegates did everything they could to see that it failed. They reasoned that if the Democrats split, the Republicans would win, and then the South would leave the Union. The party met again in Baltimore, and again there was trouble. The southern delegates walked out and chose Senator John Breckinridge of Kentucky as their candidate. Northern delegates chose Senator Stephen Douglas of Illinois.

The Republicans then met in Chicago. Senator William Seward of New York led at first, but on the third ballot, Abraham Lincoln won the nomination. The Republican platform promised homesteads, a railroad to the Pacific, and tariff protection for American industries. On slavery, the platform opposed interference with slavery in the states and called John Brown's raid a crime. In the border states, many did not like any of the choices. They formed the Constitutional Union party and chose Senator John Bell (Kentucky). They favored the Union and enforcement of the laws.

Abraham Lincoln

During the campaign, southern newspapers warned that a Lincoln election would result in the South leaving the Union. The Republicans said that they were just repeating the same threats they had used in 1856. In the North, the contest was mostly between Lincoln and Douglas. In the South, it was between Douglas and Breckinridge. In border states from Missouri to Maryland, the strongest support was for Bell or Douglas. In those days, it was considered improper for candidates to go out and give speeches, so campaigns were carried on by big rallies, parades, and speeches by supporters. When it appeared that Lincoln was going to win, Douglas ignored tradition and started campaigning in the South. He urged the South to stay in the Union, regardless of how the election turned out.

Lincoln easily won the election with 180 electoral votes—his opponents, all together, had only 123 (Breckinridge, 72; Bell, 39; Douglas, 12). In popular votes Lincoln had 1.8 million compared with 2.8 million for all opponents. When the news of Lincoln's election reached South Carolina, the legislature called for a convention to decide whether the state should secede (leave the Union). Six other states prepared to hold conventions after South Carolina acted. On December 20, 1860, South Carolina voted to leave the Union. In other states of the Deep South, this was a signal to act.

RESULTS: South Carolina, by its own action, was now an "independent nation." It was not alone for long, however. Six states joined it, and in a meeting in Montgomery, Alabama, the Confederate States of America was formed. Jefferson Davis was elected provisional president. Everyone waited now to see how Lincoln would react.

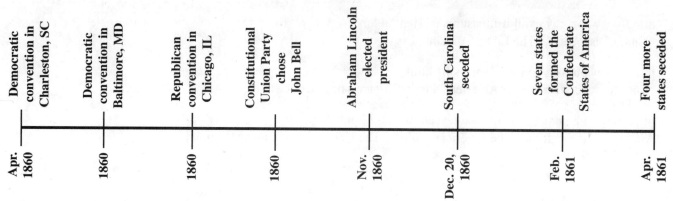

Democratic convention in Charleston, SC	Democratic convention in Baltimore, MD	Republican convention in Chicago, IL	Constitutional Union Party chose John Bell	Abraham Lincoln elected president	South Carolina seceded	Seven states formed the Confederate States of America	Four more states seceded
Apr. 1860	1860	1860	1860	Nov. 1860	Dec. 20, 1860	Feb. 1861	Apr. 1861

Name: _____ Date: _____

South Carolina Secedes: Reinforcement

Directions: Complete the following activities, essays, and challenges on your own paper.

ACTIVITIES:

1. Examine a map and locate the original seven Confederate States of America (CSA): Alabama, Florida, Georgia, Louisiana, Mississippi, South Carolina, and Texas. How easily would it have been for those states to have defended themselves?
2. Discuss why Lincoln's election was so upsetting to the South.

ESSAYS:

1. Among themselves, Lincoln's rivals had many more popular votes than he had. If his rivals had all worked to choose Douglas, could he have won? Why?
2. In your view, was there any way that Lincoln could have done anything that would have changed the South's mind about him or his party? Why?
3. If a group of states bordering yours was to secede from the United States, what kinds of problems would they face?

CHALLENGES:

1. Why did southern delegates at the Democratic convention cause so much trouble?
2. Who did southerners choose for president in 1860?
3. Who did northern Democrats pick in 1860?
4. Who was Lincoln's closest rival for the Republican nomination?
5. How did the Republican platform appeal for support from Californians?
6. Where was Bell's support strongest?
7. Why did Douglas campaign in the South when he knew Lincoln was going to win?
8. In electoral votes, how far behind Lincoln was his nearest rival?
9. How many more people voted for Lincoln's rivals than voted for him?
10. How many states were represented when the Confederate States of America was formed?

NATIONAL STANDARDS CORRELATIONS:

NCSS VIf: (Power, Authority, & Governance) Explain conditions, actions, and motivations that contribute to conflict and cooperation within and among nations.
NSH Era 5, Standard 1: The causes of the Civil War

WEBSITES:

http://www.loc.gov/exhibits/treasures/tr11b.html#civil
"Union Dissolved!," The Library of Congress

http://www.pbs.org/civilwar/war/map1.html
"The Confederate States of America," Public Broadcasting Service

http://www.lib.uchicago.edu/e/spcl/excat/douglas7.html
"Stephen A. Douglas and the American Union," The University of Chicago Library

Lincoln Asks for 75,000 Volunteers

P. G. T. Beauregard

March 4, 1861, finally arrived, and for tired, worn President Buchanan, it was not quickly enough. Seven states had left the Union and had formed the Confederacy (CSA). U.S. forts and arsenals were taken by the states, and southern militia units were drilling on a regular basis. Only Ft. Sumter in Charleston harbor and Ft. Pickens off the Florida coast remained in U.S. hands. Still, no one knew whether there would be a war. Some in the North were willing to let the South go peacefully, but no one was sure what President-elect Abraham Lincoln would do. On his trip from Springfield, Illinois, to Washington, he made no statement hinting at what his policy would be. The nation waited nervously to see if Lincoln's policy would bring peace or war.

In words carefully chosen, Lincoln said in his inaugural address, "In *your* hands, my dissatisfied fellow countrymen, and not in *mine*, is the momentous issue of civil war. The government will not assail *you*. You can have no conflict without being yourselves the aggressors." In other words, there would not be a war unless the South started it.

The nation's attention focused on Ft. Sumter, commanded by Colonel Robert Anderson from Kentucky. He had quietly removed the small garrison from Ft. Moultrie, across the harbor from Ft. Sumter, but he knew that unless food and other supplies were sent, he could not hold out for long. A relief ship, *Star of the West*, had tried to reach Ft. Sumter in January but had turned back after being hit by South Carolina militia cannons. No effort was made to send supplies by Buchanan. The new Confederate government sent General P.G.T. Beauregard to Charleston to take command. By the time Lincoln became president, Ft. Sumter was almost out of food. To supply the fort meant certain war; not to supply it would be to hand it over without a fight. When Beauregard sent officers to the fort, Anderson told them he could not hold out much longer, but the South knew relief ships were on the way. On April 12, 1861, Confederate guns opened fire on Ft. Sumter, and two days later, Anderson surrendered. The Confederate flag flew over the fort, and Anderson and his men were allowed to leave.

Lincoln acted quickly and called on the nation's governors to send 75,000 militia to serve three-month terms as federal soldiers. In border states, governors were put on the spot. In the states of the Upper South (Virginia, Tennessee, North Carolina, and Arkansas), the governors said they would never think of fighting their friends to the South, and they and their states left the Union. Missouri's governor wanted to secede, but the Union army chased him and his friends out of the state. Maryland also had strong southern sentiment, but federal troops took control. Kentucky was so divided that it decided to stay neutral and warned both sides against sending an army into the state. Delaware was Unionist all the way.

RESULTS: As states decided which way to go, individuals also made decisions. For Colonel Robert E. Lee, deciding was especially painful. He did not approve of slavery or secession. He was offered command of the U.S. Army but turned it down. He was a Virginian, and when his state left the Union, he and many like him offered their services to the Confederacy.

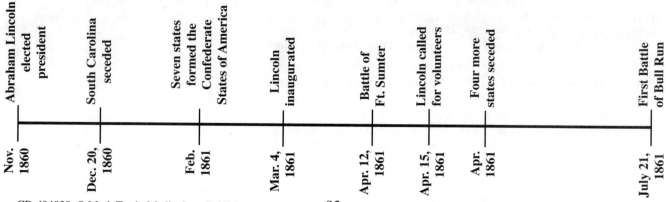

Abraham Lincoln elected president	South Carolina seceded	Seven states formed the Confederate States of America	Lincoln inaugurated	Battle of Ft. Sumter	Lincoln called for volunteers	Four more states seceded	First Battle of Bull Run
Nov. 1860	Dec. 20, 1860	Feb. 1861	Mar. 4, 1861	Apr. 12, 1861	Apr. 15, 1861	Apr. 1861	July 21, 1861

Name: _____ Date: _____

Lincoln Asks for 75,000 Volunteers: Reinforcement

Directions: Complete the following activities, essays, and challenges on your own paper.

ACTIVITIES:

1. After checking an almanac, total up the land area of the Confederate States of America, as well as the United States above the seceding states in 1860. If land was the key, which side would win?
2. As a border-state resident in 1861, debate whether your state should leave the Union after the firing on Ft. Sumter.

ESSAYS:

1. What do you think went on in the governors' minds when they were told to send militia units? Why?
2. If you were going to blame someone for starting the fighting, would you blame Lincoln or the Confederates for it? Why?
3. Putting yourself in Robert E. Lee's shoes, what would you have done? Why?

CHALLENGES:

1. What two forts in the South remained in U.S. hands when Lincoln became president?
2. How much did the public know about Lincoln's attitude toward Southern secession and if he favored war?
3. In his inaugural address, how did Lincoln try to avoid any blame for anything that might happen?
4. Why was the *Star of the West* sent to Ft. Sumter? Why did it turn back?
5. Why was General Beauregard sent to Charleston?
6. Why didn't Beauregard wait when he knew Anderson was short on food?
7. On what day did the Stars and Bars (Confederate flag) rise over Ft. Sumter?
8. What four states left the Union after Lincoln called for 75,000 volunteers?
9. What four slave states did not leave the Union?
10. What reasons might Robert E. Lee have given for staying in the U.S. Army?

NATIONAL STANDARDS CORRELATIONS:

NCSS Xf: (Civic Ideals & Practices) Identify and explain the roles of formal and informal political actors in influencing and shaping public policy and decision-making.
NSH Era 5, Standard 1: The causes of the Civil War

WEBSITES:

http://memory.loc.gov/cgi-bin/query/r?ammem/mal:@field(DOCID+@lit(d0807400))
"Abraham Lincoln, Monday, April 15, 1861 (Proclamation on State Militia)," The Library of Congress

http://www.loc.gov/exhibits/treasures/tr11b.html#civil
"Memory Gallery B: A More Perfect Union," The Library of Congress

http://www.nps.gov/liho/secession.htm
"Lincoln on Secession," National Park Service

http://www.nps.gov/gwmp/arl_hse.html
"Welcome to the Robert E. Lee Memorial," National Park Service

African-Americans Become Part of the War

Robert Shaw

In 1861, there were about 500,000 free African-Americans in the United States, almost half of those living in the North. Among them was Frederick Douglass, who had escaped from slavery. Others were freed by their masters, bought freedom, came north over the Underground Railroad, or were born in the North. Most of them lived in cities and had developed churches, clubs, and schools. Education was very important to them, and some even attended college. In the South, some free African-Americans were prosperous, but most free African-Americans in both the North and South were poor. They all knew they would never feel free until slavery was no more.

Lincoln agreed that slavery should end, but he resisted pressures by abolitionists and African-Americans to be rushed into acting too soon. He faced several complicated problems. PRIMARY OBJECTIVES: To him, the question of freeing slaves was less important than saving the Union. If the South won the war, slavery would go on as before. MILITARY: Four border slave states had remained in the Union: Missouri, Maryland, Kentucky, and Delaware. By acting too soon, opinion in those states would turn against the Union. If they left the Union, the war could be lost. LEGAL: The Constitution said that private property could not be taken without just compensation to the owner. He tried to talk some slave state leaders into giving up slavery in return for $400 per slave. They turned him down.

Meanwhile, African-Americans were helping the war effort on both sides. Southern African-Americans produced food, acted as servants for soldiers, and built fortifications. Many northern African-Americans wanted to enlist in the army but were turned down. However, officers in the field began using runaway slaves as workers. General Ben Butler called them "contraband of war," and after that, they were often referred to as "contrabands."

Waiting until after the North won a major battle (so it would not look like a desperate measure), Lincoln issued a preliminary Emancipation Proclamation, saying that on January 1, 1863, "All persons held as slaves within any state [still in rebellion] shall be ... forever free." Since the South was using slaves in its war effort, he justified ending slavery as a war measure. It did not satisfy some abolitionists, and it angered the South.

Some Union officers began using African-Americans as soldiers before it was government policy. The first unit officially approved was the 1st South Carolina Volunteers commanded by Colonel Thomas Higginson. The most famous African-American unit was the 54th Massachusetts, led by Colonel Robert Shaw.

African-American soldiers were paid less than whites, were often used as labor details, and were the most poorly equipped. Despite this, desertions were very rare, and they performed well in battle. In 1863 at Ft. Wagner, South Carolina, 247 of Shaw's men were killed out of the unit's 600 men. Sixteen African-American soldiers received the Congressional Medal of Honor.

Confederate Major General Patrick Cleburne suggested in 1863, African-Americans be recruited. The idea was turned down at the time, but in 1865, General Lee suggested it, and it was accepted. By that time, however, the war was lost.

RESULTS: In 1865, the passing of the Thirteenth Amendment ended all slavery in America.

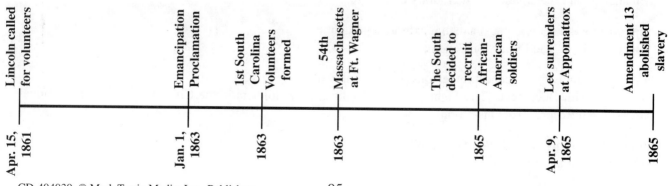

Lincoln called for volunteers	Emancipation Proclamation	1st South Carolina Volunteers formed	54th Massachusetts at Ft. Wagner	The South decided to recruit African-American soldiers	Lee surrenders at Appomattox	Amendment 13 abolished slavery
Apr. 15, 1861	Jan. 1, 1863	1863	1863	1865	Apr. 9, 1865	1865

Name: _____ Date: _____

African-Americans Become Part of the War: Reinforcement

Directions: Complete the following activities, essays, and challenges on your own paper.

ACTIVITIES:

1. Examine a map and have the class list problems Lincoln would have faced if Missouri, Maryland, and Kentucky had left the Union. In light of that, does the class think he was wise to wait to issue the Emancipation Proclamation?
2. Show part of the movie *Glory* in class. Ask students to list problems the men in the 54th Massachusetts faced.

ESSAYS:

1. As an abolitionist, would you be pleased with the Emancipation Proclamation just announced by President Lincoln? Why?
2. If you were an escaped slave living in the North, would you be enthusiastic about joining the army? Why?
3. If you were a slave in the South in 1865, and were told you could have freedom if you joined the Confederate army, would you have joined?

CHALLENGES:

1. What were some of the ways in which slaves had gained freedom before the Emancipation Proclamation?
2. Where did most northern African-Americans live?
3. Why did Lincoln put saving the Union ahead of ending slavery?
4. If Missouri and Kentucky had left the Union, which rivers would have separated the North from the South?
5. How much did Lincoln want to pay loyal slaveowners for their slaves? What happened to the idea?
6. Who first referred to escaped slaves as "contrabands"?
7. How did Lincoln justify taking slaves away from their masters?
8. Name two colonels commanding African-American troops.
9. How many men of the 54th Massachusetts were killed in one battle?
10. Who first proposed that African-American troops serve in the Confederate army?

NATIONAL STANDARDS CORRELATIONS:

NCSS IVb: (Individual Development & Identity) Describe personal connections to place—as associated with community, nation, and world.
NSH Era 5, Standard 2: The course and character of the Civil War and its effects on the American people

WEBSITES:

http://memory.loc.gov/ammem/alhtml/almintr.html
"Emancipation Proclamation," The Library of Congress

http://memory.loc.gov/ammem/aaohtml/exhibit/aopart4.html
"The Civil War," The Library of Congress

http://www.archives.gov/education/lessons/blacks-civil-war/
"Teaching With Documents: The Fight for Equal Rights: Black Soldiers in the Civil War," The U.S. National Archives and Records Administration

http://www.pbs.org/wgbh/aia/part4/4p2967.html
"The Civil War and Emancipation," Public Broadcasting Service

The South Scores Some Wins

Statistics seemed to show that the Confederacy did not have any chance of winning the Civil War. They were outnumbered 10–1 in manufacturing, 3–1 in miles of railroad, and 2–1 in manpower. Their roads and railroads were much worse than those in the North. Despite the odds, the South thought they could win. At times, it looked as if they might be able to win just enough so the North would give them independence.

The South had a few things going for it. Most of the time, Southerners were fighting on familiar land with many civilians keeping them informed on what the Union army was doing. They also had many fine officers who had been trained at West Point and southern military schools. Among these were Robert E. Lee, Thomas (Stonewall) Jackson, Joseph Johnston, James Longstreet, and J.E.B. Stuart. At the beginning of the war, both armies were almost equally armed and neither had previous battlefield experience.

Robert E. Lee

After the attack on Ft. Sumter in April 1861, both sides raised large armies. Commanding the North's Army of the Potomac was General Irwin McDowell; the South's Army of Northern Virginia was led by General P.G.T. Beauregard. The two armies met at Bull Run, and it seemed like a Union victory until Stonewall Jackson's fresh Confederate troops arrived. The Union army broke under the pressure and rushed back to Washington. The southern troops did not pursue, which made President Jefferson Davis angry.

McDowell was replaced by General George McClellan, a careful man who did not want to fight until victory was certain. Rather than move by land toward Richmond, he transported his army by boat to the James Peninsula, southeast of Richmond. The Confederate general preparing to defend the city was Joe Johnston. When Johnston was wounded, General Robert E. Lee replaced him. Lee sent Jackson toward the North to keep Lincoln from sending more men to McClellan. Jackson's men moved so fast that they were known as "foot cavalry," and that caused Union troops to be sent after him. Lee then attacked in the Seven Days' Campaign. As McClellan left the Peninsula, Lee had to turn quickly to face a new army, that of John Pope. The two armies fought the Second Battle of Bull Run, and again the South won.

McClellan was again appointed commander of the Union army. Lee's army moved north into western Maryland. After Union soldiers found a copy of Lee's orders wrapped around three cigars, McClellan sent his army to meet the Confederates at Antietam Creek. In a bloody battle that left 25,000 men dead or wounded, the Confederates withdrew across the Potomac River to Virginia. Because McClellan did not attack Lee's army as they retreated, McClellan was fired. General Ambrose Burnside replaced him.

RESULTS: Burnside planned to move quickly across the Rappahannock River at Fredericksburg, but the pontoons he needed for the bridge did not arrive when they were expected. When they did cross the river, the Confederates were well prepared, and the Union soldiers were badly beaten. Joe Hooker replaced Burnside, and the two armies met again at Chancellorsville. In a daring move, Lee split his outnumbered army and hit Hooker's flank. The Union army headed north in defeat.

Directions: Complete the following activities, essays, and challenges on your own paper.

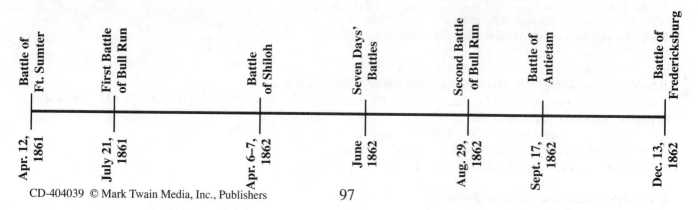

Battle of Ft. Sumter	First Battle of Bull Run	Battle of Shiloh	Seven Days' Battles	Second Battle of Bull Run	Battle of Antietam	Battle of Fredericksburg
Apr. 12, 1861	July 21, 1861	Apr. 6–7, 1862	June 1862	Aug. 29, 1862	Sept. 17, 1862	Dec. 13, 1862

Name: _____ Date: _____

The South Scores Some Wins: Reinforcement

ACTIVITIES:

1. Make a list of Union generals who faced Lee and the battles they fought.
2. Research Civil War generals, and use the information to create fact cards.

ESSAYS:

1. After looking up the words *infantry*, *cavalry*, and *artillery*, tell why you think each of them would be important in fighting a Civil War battle.
2. As a Union soldier in the Civil War, how would you feel about the way the army was being handled? Give examples.
3. *Morale* is a term often used in describing the attitude of a soldier or an athlete. If the Union army were a basketball team at your school, what would its morale have been after playing the first few "games" during the war?

CHALLENGES:

1. In what way did the North have the greatest advantage over the South?
2. What was the first major land battle of the war?
3. What were two advantages the South had in the war?
4. What happened at Bull Run that gave Confederates the victory?
5. Why was Beauregard in trouble even though he won at Bull Run?
6. How did Lee manage to keep McClellan's army from being even larger than it already was?
7. How did it happen that Lee replaced Johnston during the Peninsular Campaign?
8. After looking up the meaning of *cavalry*, why do you suppose Stonewall Jackson's men were called "foot cavalry"?
9. Why was McClellan in trouble with Lincoln after he won at Antietam?
10. Lee had a low opinion of Hooker as a general. Even though Lee's army was outnumbered 2–1, what did he do at Chancellorsville that indicated his attitude toward Hooker?

NATIONAL STANDARDS CORRELATIONS:

NCSS VId: (Power, Authority, & Governance) Describe the ways nations and organizations respond to forces of unity and diversity affecting order and security.

NSH Era 5, Standard 2: The course and character of the Civil War and its effects on the American people

WEBSITES:

http://www.nps.gov/anti/battle.htm
"Battlefield Information," National Park Service

http://www.nps.gov/anti/casualty.htm
"Casualties at Antietam," National Park Service

http://www.swcivilwar.com/LincolnLetMacAntietam.html
"Lincoln's Letter to George McClellan after Antietam," The Snuff Works

http://www.nps.gov/frsp/chist.htm
"The Battle of Chancellorsville," National Park Service

July 4, 1863—A Day of Northern Victories

Ulysses S. Grant

While much of the nation's attention was on Union defeats in Virginia, a Union general in the West was gaining a reputation for winning—Ulysses Grant, a West Point graduate who had left the army in 1854. When the war began, he was working at his father's hardware store. He was appointed a colonel in the Illinois infantry, but he soon showed an ability to win battles. Victories at Ft. Henry and Ft. Donelson gave the Union control of the Tennessee River and something to cheer about. Lincoln made him a major general. During the Battle of Shiloh, he was able to take an army that had been badly mauled, turn it around, and win. In each of these battles, the navy helped him. His next assignment was much more difficult—to capture the city of Vicksburg, Mississippi. Sitting on a high bluff across the Mississippi River from a low, swampy area, Vicksburg was important because it was the only link still in Confederate hands between the western and eastern parts of the Confederacy. It could not be approached without the enemy knowing about it, and early efforts had failed.

In 1863, Grant moved his army southward into Louisiana on the west side of the river. A fleet under Admiral David Porter blasted its way past Vicksburg and joined Grant far south of Vicksburg. Protected by gunboats, Grant's army crossed into Mississippi, captured the capital at Jackson, then turned westward to attack Vicksburg from the rear. The city was besieged. Exploding shells forced residents to live in caves. Food ran low, and people lived by eating cats, dogs, and mules. Finally, on July 4, 1863, General John Pemberton surrendered, and 30,000 soldiers were captured.

In 1863, the Confederate government approved Lee's plan to invade Pennsylvania. It might relieve pressure on Vicksburg, encourage the northern peace movement, and feed the army at the North's expense. The army had been so successful that any doubts were removed that they could go all the way to Harrisburg and even capture Washington. With an army 75,000 men strong, the Army of Northern Virginia headed northward.

On June 28, 1863, Lincoln replaced Joe Hooker with General George Meade. By then, southern troops had reached Chambersburg and York and were near Harrisburg. No one planned to fight at Gettysburg, but on July 1, Confederate troops met strong resistance there, and messages were sent by both sides to their commanders. Troops were rushed to this quiet town, and the greatest battle ever fought in North America was shaping up.

The Union Army held Cemetery Ridge, and Lee was determined to drive them off. The greatest effort took place July 3, when 15,000 men crossed the field toward the Union line in the famous Pickett's Charge. About 7,000 men were lost in the attempt. On July 4, Lee expected the North to attack, but when nothing happened, he began his withdrawal. Because of high water, he could not cross the Potomac River until July 13. The next day, when most of the Confederates were across the river, Meade attacked, but it was too late to do much harm.

RESULTS: The Confederates were badly bruised, but still dangerous. The war would continue nearly two more years, but the South had lost too many men to ever again take the offensive.

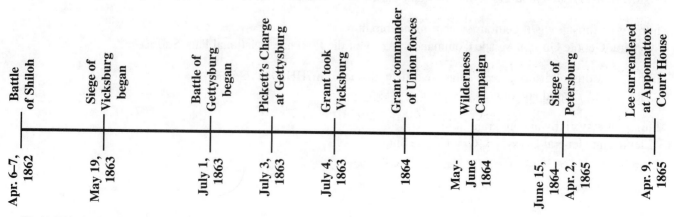

Battle of Shiloh	Siege of Vicksburg began	Battle of Gettysburg began	Pickett's Charge at Gettysburg	Grant took Vicksburg	Grant commander of Union forces	Wilderness Campaign	Siege of Petersburg	Lee surrendered at Appomattox Court House
Apr. 6–7, 1862	May 19, 1863	July 1, 1863	July 3, 1863	July 4, 1863	1864	May–June 1864	June 15, 1864– Apr. 2, 1865	Apr. 9, 1865

Name: _____ Date: _____

July 4, 1863—A Day of Northern Victories: Reinforcement

Directions: Complete the following activities, essays, and challenges on your own paper.

ACTIVITIES:

1. Discuss how modern people would suffer during a siege. If your city were surrounded, from what shortages would you suffer? What changes would there be to your lifestyle?
2. Examine maps of the Gettysburg battlefield. Discuss how Pickett's Charge would appear to southern and northern soldiers watching it.

ESSAYS:

1. General Lee rode out to meet Pickett's men as they came back from the battle and told them it was all his fault. Research the battle and give your opinion of what went wrong.
2. You are President Lincoln. Write a letter that you would send to General Grant after the battle at Vicksburg.
3. You are President Lincoln. Write a letter that you would send to General Meade on July 15.

CHALLENGES:

1. What were three battles that made Grant famous?
2. Why was Vicksburg hard to capture?
3. Why was Vicksburg important?
4. How did Grant attack Vicksburg?
5. How did the people of Vicksburg survive the siege?
6. How many men did Lee have in his army when he invaded Pennsylvania?
7. Before the first skirmish at Gettysburg, how long had Meade been in charge of the Union army?
8. What was the most important day of the battle, and what made it so special?
9. How was Lee able to escape?
10. Why didn't the South ever go on the offensive again?

NATIONAL STANDARDS CORRELATIONS:

NCSS VId: (Power, Authority, & Governance) Describe the ways nations and organizations respond to forces of unity and diversity affecting order and security.
NSH Era 5, Standard 2: The course and character of the Civil War and its effects on the American people

WEBSITES:

http://www.nps.gov/gett/gettkidz/kidzindex.htm
"'Hey, Ranger!' Gettysburg National Military Park's Civil War Page for Kids!," National Park Service

http://www.nps.gov/gett/getttour/sidebar/meadebio.htm
"General George Gordon Meade Commander, Army of the Potomac," National Park Service

http://www.digitalhistory.uh.edu/database/article_display.cfm?HHID=116
"Vicksburg," Digital History

http://www.swcivilwar.com/grant.html
"Lieutenant General Ulysses S. Grant," The Snuff Works

Women Join the War Effort on Both Sides

Belle Boyd

As soldiers went off to war, they often sang of "The Girl I Left Behind," and love ballads like "Lorena" and "Aura Lee" were popular with both armies in the Civil War. It was Julia Ward Howe who inspired Union troops with "The Battle Hymn of the Republic."

Women were not supposed to be part of war, but they were as patriotic and enthusiastic as the men. John Milton had written: "They also serve who only stand and wait." These women were determined to do more than stand and wait. They would help. Women took over the farms, doing the chores their husbands had always done. Women went to work in factories to produce arms and clothing needed by the armies. Before this time, it had not been proper for a "lady" to do much of the work that necessity now required.

Some women became active participants in the war. Women spies were used by both sides, and some became famous. Rose Greenhow lived in Washington and knew many government officials. She sent General Beauregard word that the Union army was moving toward Bull Run. She was captured and held prisoner for a while. Belle Boyd often went through Union lines carrying information to Stonewall Jackson and medicine for his troops. She was arrested six times and put in prison twice. During the war, many other women reported Union troop movements to Confederate officers. A few women even disguised themselves as men and enlisted in the army.

Of northern spies, the most important was Elizabeth Van Lew, who lived in Richmond and gathered information from Union prisoners held at Libby Prison. She was even able to plant one of her former slaves, Mary Bowser, as a servant at Jefferson Davis's home. Her information to General Grant was very useful, and when his army entered Richmond, he stopped at her home for tea.

Taking care of the soldiers' needs was a common activity of women. Those in Richmond often opened their homes to soldiers in need of a home-cooked meal. After a battle, homes in the area became field hospitals for wounded and sick soldiers. Nursing wounded soldiers was a common activity among southern women during the war. Because the South was short on medical supplies, food, and doctors, their role was crucial in saving many lives. Some northern women were best known for their role in nursing. Dorothea Dix was Superintendent of United States Army Nurses, with a rank equal to that of a major general. When she saw the needs of soldiers, she issued appeals for bed shirts, preserves, and canned goods. Every request she made for supplies was more than met by donations from all over the North. She came down on hospital superintendents who mistreated the men, and one was advised: "If you have her down on you, you might as well have hell after you." Clara Barton became famous as a battlefield nurse (and later founded the American Red Cross). Mary "Mother" Bickerdyke was a widow in her forties who devoted great efforts to taking care of enlisted men. She was hated by lazy, cruel, incompetent doctors, but it did them no good to complain. General Grant and General Sherman admired her and were always on her side.

RESULTS: Women made important contributions to the war effort in both the North and the South. For the first time, women began to experience a sense of independence and accomplishment that would not be forgotten after the war. Women were beginning to see that they could make valuable contributions to their families and the nation in careers outside the home.

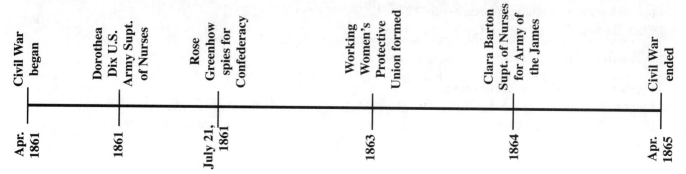

Civil War began — Apr. 1861

Dorothea Dix U.S. Army Supt. of Nurses — 1861

Rose Greenhow spies for Confederacy — July 21, 1861

Working Women's Protective Union formed — 1863

Clara Barton Supt. of Nurses for Army of the James — 1864

Civil War ended — Apr. 1865

Name: _____ Date: _____

Women Join the War Effort on Both Sides: Reinforcement

Directions: Complete the following activities, essays, and challenges on your own paper.

ACTIVITIES:

1. Devise a code that would be simple to use but hard to break.
2. Discuss some of the difficult situations that volunteer nurses may have had to face.

ESSAYS:

1. How were female spies more effective many times than male spies?
2. You are a soldier's wife writing about events at home. You don't want to worry your husband, but you want him to know you and the children are having a hard time surviving without him. Write the letter.
3. You are a wounded soldier. How would the presence of women acting as nurses help you feel better?

CHALLENGES:

1. What did women do during the war that they had not done before?
2. Why was Clara Barton more important after the war than during it?
3. Why weren't doctors always happy with women like Miss Dix or Mrs. Bickerdyke?

What part did each of the following women play in the war?

4. Rose Greenhow
5. Mary Bowser
6. Belle Boyd
7. Elizabeth Van Lew
8. Dorothea Dix
9. "Mother" Bickerdyke
10. Julia Ward Howe

NATIONAL STANDARDS CORRELATIONS:

<u>**NCSS IVg:**</u> (Individual Development & Identity) Identify and interpret examples of stereotyping, conformity, and altruism.
<u>**NSH Era 5, Standard 2:**</u> The course and character of the Civil War and its effects on the American people

WEBSITES:

http://www.womensmemorial.org/historyandcollections/history/lrnmreearlycivil.html
"Early Years: the Civil War," Women in Military Service for America Memorial Foundation, Inc.

http://www.loc.gov/exhibits/treasures/trm072.html
"Clara Barton," The Library of Congress

http://scriptorium.lib.duke.edu/women/cwdocs.html
"Civil War Women: Primary Sources on the Internet," Library Duke University

http://www.archives.gov/publications/prologue/1993/spring/women-in-the-civil-war-3.html
"Women Soldiers of the Civil War, Part 3," The U.S. National Archives and Records Administration

Booth Kills Lincoln

John Wilkes Booth

After defeats at Vicksburg and Gettysburg, friends of the South watched events unfold with greater gloom. After Vicksburg, Grant had defeated the South at Chattanooga and was then appointed supreme commander of Union forces. He took command of the Army of the Potomac and assigned William T. Sherman the task of marching to Atlanta and then from Atlanta to the coast. When Joe Johnston could not stop the advance, President Davis replaced him with John Hood. Hood lost Atlanta in September 1864, and Sherman made a path 60 miles wide to the coast, arriving in Savannah on December 22, 1864. The South, divided at the Mississippi in 1863, had been divided again. Meanwhile, Grant was conducting a relentless campaign that began with the Wilderness in May 1864; ignoring enormous losses, he pinned Lee's army down in the trenches at Petersburg.

Also devastating to Confederate supporters was Lincoln's reelection in 1864. During the war, a group of Democrats called "Copperheads" tried to stir up opposition to the war and to Lincoln. They had counted on the 1864 election as a way for those who did not like the war, the draft, the Emancipation Proclamation, or Lincoln to defeat him by electing McClellan. When Lincoln won, most accepted it. John Wilkes Booth did not, however.

Booth was the son of famous actor Junius Booth and grew up in a stage-struck family. John Wilkes wasn't as impressed with the lines of Shakespeare's plays as with the action. He didn't walk onto stage; he jumped. In swordfighting scenes, he was so intense that he often injured his opponent. He sometimes leaped from boulders on the stage to give greater effect. He loved plays with sinister plots and high drama. He was popular with the ladies and with a strange assortment of admiring misfits. Among these were Lewis Powell (a man who was tall, strong, and illiterate) and George Atzerodt (a cowardly man, but a skilled boatman).

When Booth was unhappy, he drank; and as news of Confederate defeats came, he was more despondent than ever. He loved the South and felt a need to do something desperate and theatrical to save it. He had plotted a kidnapping of Lincoln in the past, but his plans never worked out. Lee's surrender at Appomattox Court House on April 9, 1865, made kidnapping useless. He had gone with the crowd to the White House on April 11 and heard Lincoln's brief and conciliatory speech that night and vowed, "That is the last speech he will ever make." His thoughts now turned to murder.

On April 14, Booth learned that Lincoln would attend Ford's Theatre that evening, and he called his friends together. Atzerodt was to kill Vice President Andrew Johnson, Powell was to kill Secretary of State Seward, and Booth would kill Lincoln. Atzerodt did nothing, but Powell broke into Seward's home and attacked him in his bed. However, Booth would have to play the leading role himself.

Sneaking into Lincoln's box at Ford's Theatre, Booth shot him from behind. In the leap from the box to the stage, his spur caught in the bunting, and he landed off-balance, breaking his leg. Shouting *"Sic semper tyrannis,"* Booth left the stage and rode off into the night.

RESULTS: John Wilkes Booth was surrounded and shot on April 24.

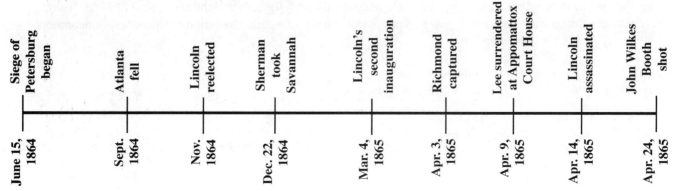

Siege of Petersburg began	Atlanta fell	Lincoln reelected	Sherman took Savannah	Lincoln's second inauguration	Richmond captured	Lee surrendered at Appomattox Court House	Lincoln assassinated	John Wilkes Booth shot
June 15, 1864	Sept. 1864	Nov. 1864	Dec. 22, 1864	Mar. 4, 1865	Apr. 3, 1865	Apr. 9, 1865	Apr. 14, 1865	Apr. 24, 1865

Name: _____ Date: _____

Booth Kills Lincoln: Reinforcement

Directions: Complete the following activities, essays, and challenges on your own paper.

ACTIVITIES:

1. Discuss how a presidential assassination affects the nation.
2. Jefferson Davis, when told of the assassination, felt sure that it would hurt the South. Discuss why he might have felt that way.

ESSAYS:

1. If Booth's plan had worked, and the president, vice president, and secretary of state had all been killed, would it have helped the South? Why or why not?
2. *Sic semper tyrannis* is Latin for "Thus always to tyrants." After reading about Lincoln, do you think Booth was thinking clearly? Why?
3. Why do you think so many presidents have been assassinated (Lincoln, Garfield, McKinley, and Kennedy), and attempts have been made on others (Jackson, Truman, Ford, and Reagan)?

CHALLENGES:

1. What two Confederate generals failed to stop Sherman?
2. Why was Sherman's march important to Union victory?
3. Who were "Copperheads"?
4. Who did Copperheads back in the 1864 election?
5. What kind of acting did John Wilkes Booth enjoy most?
6. Who were some of his friends?
7. When did Booth decide to kill Lincoln?
8. What were Atzerodt's and Powell's assignments on April 14, 1865?
9. How did Booth break his leg?
10. How long did the search for Booth take?

NATIONAL STANDARDS CORRELATIONS:

NCSS Xf: (Civic Ideals & Practices) Identify and explain the roles of formal and informal political actors in influencing and shaping public policy and decision-making.
NSH Era 5, Standard 2: The course and character of the Civil War and its effects on the American people

WEBSITES:

http://www.cviog.uga.edu/Projects/gainfo/marchsea.htm
"Sherman's March to the Sea," Carl Vinson Institute of Government, University of Georgia

http://www.law.umkc.edu/faculty/projects/ftrials/lincolnconspiracy/lincolnnews.html
"Newspaper Accounts of the Lincoln Assassination, Conspiracy Trial, and Execution of Convicted Conspirators," University of Missouri–Kansas City

http://memory.loc.gov/ammem/today/mar11.html
"Today in History: March 11," The Library of Congress

http://www.lib.niu.edu/ipo/iht319615.html
"Copperheads," Illinois Periodicals Online

Name: _____ Date: _____

The Bragging Contest

At a convention of famous people of the past, who could make the following statements about themselves and be perfectly honest? Place the name of the correct speaker on the line next to the statement.

CONVENTION ROOM A

_____ 1. They called me "Admiral of the Ocean Seas."

_____ 2. My father wanted to cut off Captain John Smith's head, but I wouldn't let him.

_____ 3. I was hired to protect the Puritans from their enemies.

_____ 4. I told people not to fuss over religion in Maryland.

_____ 5. My attacks on Governor Cosby sure made him mad.

_____ 6. I told General Braddock what to do, but he didn't listen.

_____ 7. Otis and others might talk about boycotting British goods, but we saw to it that no one bought them.

_____ 8. When I throw a tea party, people really howl.

_____ 9. Born free, I was hired out by my poor parents.

_____ 10. When I said, "Give me liberty," I meant it!

_____ 11. Everyone was too serious when they signed the Declaration of Independence, so I tried to lighten things up.

_____ 12. I called deserters "sunshine patriots."

_____ 13. If it weren't for Hon Yost, I might have won.

_____ 14. The 20,000 pounds sterling looked good at first.

_____ 15. I did not trust Vergennes to put America's interests above France's, and I was right.

_____ 16. I tried to create a League of Friendship that would work, but people said later that it was a failure.

_____ 17. I tried to shut down Massachusetts courts, but the state shut me down and chased me out.

_____ 18. The idea of a meeting at Philadelphia was mine, and I am very proud of it.

GUESTS IN CONVENTION ROOM A

Sam Adams	An apprentice	Benedict Arnold
Lord Baltimore	Christopher Columbus	John Dickinson
Ben Franklin	Alexander Hamilton	Patrick Henry
John Jay	Thomas Paine	Pocahontas
Barry St. Leger	Daniel Shays	A Son of Liberty
Miles Standish	George Washington	John P. Zenger

Name: _____ Date: _____

The Bragging Contest

At a convention of famous people of the past, who could make the following statements about themselves and be perfectly honest? Place the name of the correct speaker on the line next to the statement.

CONVENTION ROOM B

_____   1.   The treaty I signed with England really made people mad at me.

_____   2.   I may have been fined $1,000, but it was worth it to make the Federal-ists lose popularity.

_____   3.   I wanted to go to court to get my commission, and the case went all the way to the Supreme Court.

_____   4.   I brought the textile industry to America.

_____   5.   I chased the French out of Haiti.

_____   6.   My *Clermont* really showed the critics up.

_____   7.   I was proud of the work my War Hawks did.

_____   8.   The Missouri Compromise was my idea.

_____   9.   As secretary of state, I was convinced that I, and not a military hero, deserved to be the next president.

_____   10.   They began construction on the National Road in 1811, while I was president.

_____   11.   They denied me the presidency in 1824, but I showed them in 1828.

_____   12.   I wrote an alphabet for my people, the Cherokees.

_____   13.   Jackson set out to ruin my bank and did it.

_____   14.   My effort in Richmond inspired Nat Turner 31 years later.

_____   15.   I was president when Congress admitted Texas to the Union.

GUESTS IN CONVENTION ROOM B

John Q. Adams	Nicholas Biddle	Henry Clay
Robert Fulton	Gabriel	Andrew Jackson
John Jay	Toussaint L'Ouverture	Matthew Lyon
James Madison	William Marbury	Sequoyah
Samuel Slater	John Tyler	Jesse Thomas

Name: _____ Date: _____

The Bragging Contest

At a convention of famous people of the past, who could make the following statements about themselves and be perfectly honest? Place the name of the correct speaker on the line next to the statement.

CONVENTION ROOM C

_____ 1. I tried to talk Congress into taking Oregon, but very few listened.

_____ 2. Everyone needs an education, and I was devoted to creating the best public school I could.

_____ 3. I talked Trist into staying even though he was told to go home by the president.

_____ 4. I plainly wrote that I have never tried the Hastings Cutoff; I'm sorry about what happened to the Donner party.

_____ 5. I dazzled them on March 7—one of the best speeches I ever gave.

_____ 6. I didn't kill Uncle Tom; it was my men who did it.

_____ 7. We southerners need to get more of our people into Kansas.

_____ 8. I was the Republican nominee for president in 1856.

_____ 9. I was the chief justice who handed down the *Dred Scott* decision.

_____ 10. I was the only candidate to ever run for president on the Constitutional Union party ticket.

_____ 11. I held out at Ft. Sumter as long as I could.

_____ 12. People thought my idea of using African-American soldiers in the Confederate army was odd, but I still like it.

_____ 13. I might have succeeded in Maryland, but some careless officer left his cigars behind.

_____ 14. I never forgave General Lee for ordering that foolish charge at Gettysburg.

_____ 15. Everyone calls me "Mother."

_____ 16. I told Booth I was in favor of kidnapping, but I had no stomach for his idea of killing the vice president.

GUESTS IN CONVENTION ROOM C

Robert Anderson	David Atchison	George Atzerodt
John Bell	Mary Bickerdyke	Patrick Cleburne
John Floyd	John Frémont	Lansford Hastings
Robert E. Lee	Simon Legree	Horace Mann
George Pickett	Winfield Scott	Roger Taney
Daniel Webster		

You Decide

Some decisions affect only the person who makes them, but some affect others as well. For example, what decision could you make that would have each of the following effects:

    A. It is good for you, and good for most other people as well.

    B. It is good for you, but harms the best interests of most other people.

    C. It is bad (or hard) for you, but might be good for others.

    D. It is bad for you, and bad for others too.

Since you have made these judgments about your own actions, try to apply them to people from the past. In which category would you put the following actions? You may want to hedge on some because:

    1. it might be good in the short run, but hurt in the long run or vice versa, and

    2. while some might benefit, another large group could be hurt. That is perfectly acceptable, and in many cases, it shows that you are really thinking about your answer.

Rate each of the decisions on the following pages on the basis of the four choices above, and think of reasons for your answer. Place the letter of one of the choices above on the line next to the decision.

Decisions 1492–1787

_____ 1. Columbus decides to enslave "Indians."

_____ 2. John Smith requires that colonists work or starve.

_____ 3. Pilgrims agree to abide by the *Mayflower Compact*.

_____ 4. Roger Williams demands religious freedom in Massachusetts and Rhode Island.

_____ 5. The jury finds Peter Zenger "not guilty."

_____ 6. General Braddock does not listen to Washington's advice.

_____ 7. Parliament passes the Quartering Act.

_____ 8. Sam Adams dumps tea in Boston Harbor.

_____ 9. Slaves and indentured servants are sent to the Colonies.

_____ 10. Patrick Henry speaks out against the Intolerable Acts.

_____ 11. The signers of the Declaration of Independence risk their lives.

_____ 12. The colonel at Trenton did not bother to learn to read English.

_____ 13. Jenny McCrae went north to see her boyfriend.

_____ 14. Benedict Arnold discussed a contract with Major Andre.

_____ 15. The British decide to give America land west to the Mississippi River.

_____ 16. The Confederation is formed without an executive to lead it.

_____ 17. Nicola suggested that Washington take over as king.

_____ 18. Confederation Congress approves the decision to hold a convention at Philadelphia.

Name: _____ Date: _____

Decisions 1787–1836

_____   1.   Washington wants neutrality in the wars between England and France.

_____   2.   Federalists push the Sedition Act through Congress.

_____   3.   Madison refuses to give Marbury his commission as justice of the peace.

_____   4.   Eli Whitney designs the first cotton gin.

_____   5.   Jefferson overcomes doubts to support the Louisiana Purchase.

_____   6.   Fulton switches from art to engineering.

_____   7.   William Henry Harrison labels the Prophet a phony magician.

_____   8.   The South changes slavery from a necessary evil to a positive good.

_____   9.   The House chooses John Q. Adams over Andrew Jackson in 1824.

_____   10.   Americans invest in canals and railroads.

_____   11.   Jackson married his wife before she got a divorce from her first husband.

_____   12.   Native Americans are forced out of the southeast and sent to Oklahoma.

_____   13.   Jackson vetoes the Bank Bill in 1832.

_____   14.   Frederick Douglass stands up to Mr. Covey.

_____   15.   Child labor is used in American factories.

_____   16.   Texans refuse to give up the Alamo.

Name: _____ Date: _____

Decisions 1837–1865

_____ 1. Mrs. Whitman and Mrs. Spalding travel to Oregon.

_____ 2. William L. Garrison and Elijah Lovejoy edit abolitionist newspapers.

_____ 3. Nicholas Trist ignores instructions and stays in Mexico.

_____ 4. Forty-niners cross the continent to find gold in California.

_____ 5. Daniel Webster supports a compromise with slaveowners.

_____ 6. Harriet Beecher Stowe attacks the "Simon Legrees" of the South.

_____ 7. Stephen Douglas proposes the Kansas-Nebraska Bill.

_____ 8. The Democrats choose James Buchanan as their nominee in 1856.

_____ 9. John Brown tries to end slavery with one swift blow.

_____ 10. Lincoln pushes the issue of Ft. Sumter.

_____ 11. African-Americans join the army even though they are treated unfairly.

_____ 12. Lincoln replaces generals after they lose a single battle.

_____ 13. Lee decides to take the war to Pennsylvania.

_____ 14. Women offer to nurse wounded and sick soldiers.

_____ 15. Booth kills Lincoln.

Answer Keys

Queen Isabella Appoints an Admiral (page 6)
1. 1451 (1492 - 41 years old)
2. 1461
3. Gold Coast of Africa
4. Moors (Moslems); The final victory was at Grenada.
5. Four (Portugal, Spain, England, Spain)
6. He would have to go and discover something worth claiming.
7. Short on experience, foreigner, rejection of concept, doubt about seaworthiness of ships, etc.
8. He thought he was near India.
9. Columbus refused to believe that it wasn't China he had found.
10. Distance, difficulty of storing enough supplies, uncertainty about where he was going, doubts about how Asians would treat him, etc.
11. Could be off in the size of the earth or the size of Asia. He was off on both. He assumed from Marco Polo's writings that Asia stretched farther east than it did. But he also used the estimate that the earth was 18,000 miles in circumference. That put his island discoveries about where Asian off-shore islands would have been.

Captain John Smith Saves Jamestown (page 8)
1. Establishing colonies was too expensive for individuals. Gilbert and Raleigh were both much richer before trying to establish a colony than they were afterward.
2. Seven (when tossed overboard, when Turks captured him, by ship captain, by Native Americans, by Jamestown, by pirates, by French)
3. Cabot didn't find any riches.
4. Sir Walter Raleigh
5. The Spanish had found gold in Mexico and Peru.
6. They were looking for gold and made no attempt to hunt or farm.
7. Pocahontas; John Rolfe
8. Rich young adventurers who expected to find wealth and return to their homes.
9. Fish
10. People didn't like to work, even if it saved their lives.

Pilgrims Write the *Mayflower Compact* (page 10)
1. Look at the first four letters of the word "Puri-tan." They wanted to purify the Church of England.
2. Look at the first seven letters of "Separat-ists." They wanted to separate from the Church of England.
3. Church of England, commonly called Anglican
4. Puritans didn't think anyone was important if they violated God's laws. So when a king did something they didn't like, they wouldn't obey. That caused trouble.
5. They were having a hard time with the Stuarts who ruled England after Elizabeth I's death.
6. They had no jobs in England and no reason to suppose that the situation would be any better there than before.
7. Miles Standish; probably from Native Americans, French, Spanish, or other outsiders
8. They named it after the port from which they had sailed.
9. Others were women and children, and they had no voice in political matters.
10. William Bradford

Religious Toleration Becomes the Law in Maryland (page 12)
1. Baltimore; it was named after Lord Baltimore.
2. Parliament (or Puritans)
3. Charles I was executed by beheading.
4. Catholics; he was Catholic himself.

5. Roger Williams
6. He established the colony of Rhode Island.
7. They could be fined. If they couldn't pay the fine, they were publicly whipped and jailed.
8. He could not vote or hold public office: in other words, his opinions could be ignored.
9. Answers will vary. Students could look in a phone book for churches.
10. Because there were no Moslems or Hindus in America at the time

The Zenger Trial and Freedom of the Press (page 14)
1. *Libel* is making false accusations in writing; *slander* is making false accusations by speaking.
2. German
3. They could be punished for saying anything the officials didn't like. Also, they were bribed by officials by being chosen to print government documents.
4. They could be disbarred by any judges they offended, but Hamilton was too prominent for judges to threaten him.
5. Bail is a way of getting the accused to court. If they don't show up for trial, they lose the bail they posted. Setting bail that high for a poor man like Zenger was a way of making him sit in jail.
6. They didn't like Cosby and cheered for Zenger.
7. They were chosen by the king or the proprietor (with the approval of the king).
8. He could easily lose; he might be fined if not disbarred for protesting the judge's rulings; he might lose more conservative clients.
9. He admitted to having published critical articles, so he had violated law, but the jury decided that because it was the truth, it could not be libel. Hamilton was the most famous lawyer of his time, so he could not be easily dismissed.
10. Zenger became an official printer for the colony; his reputation was obviously not hurt badly.

Colonists Develop a Diverse Work Force (page 16)
1. The main occupation was simple farming; farmers then didn't need complex information. (It should be pointed out to students that farming today is much different and requires much schooling as well.)
2. Indentured servant. (You might point out that some indentureds were children kidnapped in port cities and forced to sign a contract with an "X.")
3. Convict servant; when Ben Franklin was told that sending them to America was to reform them, he said America should send rattlesnakes to England for their reform.
4. Strength, her ability to bear children, domestic skills, beauty, age, health, etc.
5. Wealth, health, security, the number of children he had, house, etc.
6. Spinster
7. They were apprenticed to farmers or tradespersons. The conditions were often very bad.
8. Building fences, hoeing (plows too heavy, and required two grown men), taking care of livestock, etc.
9. Milking, sewing, gardening, cooking, washing, babysitting siblings
10. They would fine them, and then they would work for the farmer who had paid their fine.

Washington Joins Braddock's Expedition (page 18)
1. His brother, Lawrence
2. 1754
3. Algonquins were French allies and therefore their enemies.
4. Possible: American farmers, English professional soldiers; Americans fighting for homes, English for pay; Americans were more used to fighting this type of war, English were more conventional types.
5. The Ohio Valley controlled the whole area from the Great Lakes south to the Ohio River; it was important for fur trade and settlers.
6. His tactic of standing and facing the enemy and then firing didn't work in a forest; Native Americans' method of fighting
7. France; Spain
8. Smaller; France had to give Canada to England and Louisiana to Spain.

9. Possible: It had tested his courage and resourcefulness: he learned that English officers were not always wise.

10. He wrote nothing—he had been killed.

James Otis Fights the Stamp Act (page 20)

1. 10,000
2. Lawyer
3. They were never enforced.
4. They had a low opinion of Americans and thought of them as children.
5. A search warrant allows the police or other government law enforcement agents to search a house or other property. The purpose is usually to find illegal or stolen items.
6. It could be used to harass him.
7. Americans had never been directly taxed by England before. They were afraid that if they gave in once, they would be taxed more in the future.
8. Americans felt great and were convinced that England had given in to their pressure. Actually, the king got tired of Grenville's lectures on the need to cut palace expenses.
9. It passed the Declaratory Act to let Americans know that even if they were not being taxed then, Parliament had every right to do it at any time.
10. Very few did; most Americans saw this as a small problem that had boiled over.

Sam Adams' Tea Party (page 22)

1. Lead, paper, glass, and tea
2. That way, they could control governors. If they caused trouble, they didn't get paid.
3. British soldiers; Americans saw them as an army of occupation.
4. To take a small incident and make something big out of it
5. If they lost American customers, they couldn't sell their products.
6. Adams was poor and needed someone with money to finance his activities. Hancock was the richest man in the Colonies.
7. It began with a snowball attack. Students might come up with a number of interesting names for it.
8. He made an engraving showing the event. Remember that in those days, there was no photojournalism.
9. East India Company
10. Unbearable; Americans felt that this was a terrible injustice, and the whole colony being severely punished was too much.

Patrick Henry Demands Liberty or Death (page 24)

1. He worked on his father's farm and hated it. (He had to pick worms off tobacco plants.)
2. They reasoned that if this could be done to one colony, it could be done to others.
3. He was told not to use the word *independence*. (It was also considered advisable to let others do the talking, so it didn't seem as if Massachusetts was the only complainer.)
4. In 1763, when he was complaining about a minister's pay. (This was known as the "Case of the Parson's Cause." Henry lost, but the jury gave the minister one pence).
5. Not much; all he had to do was pass the exam (Anyone who knew Latin and Greek would probably be allowed to practice.)
6. The House of Burgesses
7. He was afraid that hotheads would cause trouble. He tried to stop it by closing the chamber.
8. "Independence"
9. The cause was not just that of one colony; all Americans were in the same boat.
10. Answers will vary.

The Declaration of Independence Is Signed (page 26)

1. Dominion: self-governing nation of British Commonwealth; acknowledges British ruler as chief of state
2. They wanted complete independence with no ties to the British empire.

3. William Dawes and Paul Revere. A poem was written about "Paul Revere's Ride" by Henry W. Longfellow.
4. He had heard that arms and powder were stored at Lexington and Concord. They found only a few supplies. The loss of men on the way back took away any value that had been gained.
5. Between New York and Vermont
6. You don't need a general if you don't have an army; you don't need an army unless you are fighting a war.
7. Richard Henry Lee
8. Many possible sayings: "A penny saved is a penny earned." "Nothing can be said to be certain except death and taxes."
9. Franklin, Adams, Adams, Jefferson
10. They would have been hanged, decapitated, and quartered.

Washington Stages a Surprise Attack on Trenton (page 28)
1. Howe; he thought it was a terrible battle.
2. There were heavy guns on the hills overlooking Boston; there were ships in the harbor that were vulnerable.
3. Washington's army was recruited from all of the states and was paid by Congress.
4. They were those who supported the Revolution only when things were going well.
5. Rain and fog covered withdrawals; they saw this as a sign that God was sparing them from defeat.
6. Washington was furious. He was so mad that he rode up and down the line waiting for someone to shoot him and get it over with.
7. He couldn't read the warning that Washington was approaching; he didn't know English. (As he lay dying, the message was read to him in German, and then he really felt badly about it.)
8. Possible answers: shortages of food, clothing, blankets, shelter, men marching barefoot in the snow
9. 1,400
10. Many whose enlistments were up stayed in the army; they had a great deal more pride.

Saratoga: Little People Mess Up Grand Plans (page 30)
1. Hon Yost, by falsely telling the Native Americans with St. Leger that a large American force was coming
2. Colonial Secretary
3. St. Leger
4. Burgoyne
5. Howe
6. Red. It was important because her fiancé recognized it.
7. By pointing out that it was the rebel capital
8. Gates
9. By surrounding the enemy, you can win by starving them out.
10. Morale is the mental state of a person. If confident, a person can do well; if a person loses morale, he or she is easily defeated.

Benedict Arnold Betrays the Cause (page 32)
1. Book salesman and pharmacist
2. French and Indian War
3. Twice–in the leg and thigh
4. Richard Montgomery
5. Guy Carleton
6. Paying Peggy Shippen's expenses
7. John Andre
8. 20,000 pounds sterling
9. West Point–the location of the U.S. Military Academy
10. The British didn't like him and considered him a traitor.

A Peace Treaty Is Made With England in 1783 (page 34)

1. John Adams
2. He was better known because of science, inventions, and almanac. The French were more willing to help when approached by Franklin than by someone else.
3. Vergennes
4. It appealed to the French image of American culture.
5. French and Indian
6. After Saratoga, they offered home rule in the British empire.
7. New England
8. He didn't trust France to put America's interests first. (Research shows he was right.)
9. They were the people who had supported England during the war. Congress was to ask the states to return the property that had been seized.
10. Mississippi River

The States Form a Confederation (page 36)

1. The states paid their salaries; it was a way to control what their delegates did.
2. *Three things it could do*. Possible answers:
   declare war and peace - needed an easy way to get a peace treaty approved;
   manage foreign affairs - had appointed diplomats who made treaties, and would need commercial connections after the war;
   maintain army and navy - had to keep fighting the war; control Native Americans - did no good to have western lands if they could not protect settlers by making treaties with Native-American tribes
3. *Three things it could not do*. Possible answers:
   no president - every country except the United States had a king, looked odd;
   no power to tax - depended on the charity of states; looked weak;
   lack of state support - states had their own problems, saw Congress as a pest;
   danger of foreign involvement - risked foreign takeover;
   danger of military takeover - soldiers still armed and organized
4. John Dickinson
5. Land Ordinance of 1785
6. None; they all had one vote.

Old Soldiers Threaten Civilian Rule (page 38)

1. Continentals
2. Gates was the general who won at Saratoga, and he gained popularity from that.
3. He suggested that Washington take over as king.
4. Congress owed them money, and they badly needed it.
5. Rhode Island
6. New Hampshire; they were saved by the militia.
7. Massachusetts
8. He put on his eyeglasses.
9. Farmers were threatened with eviction for not paying taxes.
10. Because they were organized and armed and knew something about tactics

The Calling of the Constitutional Convention (page 40)

1. Alexander Hamilton; it was called to correct defects in the Articles of Confederation.
2. England, France, and Spain were all causing the Confederation problems.
3. George Washington's
4. Ben Franklin (His legs caused him trouble, so he was taken to sessions in a chair carried by four inmates of the local jail.)

5. James Madison; they were important to historians because the official records were sketchy. (Madison told others he would keep the notes secret; they were not published until after his death.)
6. Republican
7. Each branch of government had the power to block any other branch from taking too much power.
8. Because of health reasons, he wanted to stay home.
9. Congress: senators and representatives, Executive: president, Judicial: Supreme Court justices
10. 17

Washington Stays Calm in Stormy Times (page 42)
1. Thomas Jefferson; the secretary of state is responsible for foreign affairs.
2. Republicans
3. He stopped the riots but didn't make martyrs out of the men he punished.
4. Powers of the president
5. He was the French minister to the United States; he ignored the neutrality law by persuading Americans to raid English ships.
6. We were a small, weak country. Getting into war would endanger American ships and cut off needed trade.
7. He did not want the job; he would have preferred to stay home on his farm.
8. The British agreed to leave forts in the northwest. (You might point out that they were only doing what they had already said they would do in the peace treaty.)
9. He did not like them and said they divided public opinion.
10. An alliance is an agreement between two or more countries to help each other in time of war. He thought a permanent arrangement would get the United States into wars it did not start and did not want.

Eli Whitney Invents the Cotton Gin (page 44)
1. 53.3 bales
2. Because tobacco lands were wearing out, and tobacco employed the most slaves
3. Removing cotton seeds from the boll
4. A college education would ruin a person who could work with his hands
5. Sea island had a longer fiber and was easier to clean.
6. Upland
7. Tobacco
8. It made it cheaper because it was more plentiful, and that lowered the price.
9. Interchangeable parts because it lowers production costs
10. Increased the need for slave labor

Matthew Lyon Defies the Sedition Act (page 46)
1. The Alien Act increased the time before a person could be a citizen from five to 14 years; it gave the president the power to expel undesirable aliens.
2. Because immigrants were joining the Republican party
3. Lyon was a member of the House of Representatives.
4. Lyon hated Adams and insulted him often in his newspaper.
5. Agents were sent by Talleyrand demanding a bribe just to talk to him.
6. They increased the army and navy and passed the Alien and Sedition Acts.
7. Lyon was found guilty and sentenced to a $1,000 fine and four months in jail.
8. Madison and Jefferson
9. Vice president
10. The Alien Act was repealed; the Sedition Act expired.

Opportunity Knocks: Jefferson Responds (page 48)
1. Napoleon
2. It was secret, and the United States did not learn about it until a year later.
3. The Spanish governor in New Orleans withdrew the right to deposit goods there.
4. $11,250,000 (Remember that the French received only three-fourths of the purchase price.)
5. The Constitution did not say anything about buying land; as a strict constructionist, this bothered Jefferson.
6. They were afraid Napoleon would back out of the deal if the United States took too much time.
7. Monroe
8. He helped by defeating the French army in Haiti. By doing that, Louisiana was useless to Napoleon.
9. Lewis and Clark
10. Loose construction; Constitution did not list acquiring land as a power of Congress but allowed it to make treaties. That authority was enough to convince Jefferson.

John Marshall Declares an Act of Congress Unconstitutional (page 50)
1. He had been a member of the House of Representatives.
2. Five
3. Federalist
4. A justice had to ride circuit and hear cases.
5. Because he and the others were chosen at the last minute by Adams
6. Judiciary Act of 1789
7. It hears cases on appeal from a larger court.
8. Disputes between states and cases involving ambassadors
9. Because they were Federalists; if they did not get the jobs, he could have given the jobs to Republicans.
10. It is the right of the court to examine a law and decide if it is within what the Constitution allows.

"Fulton's Folly" Changes Transportation (page 52)
1. Pencils, skyrockets, paddlewheel
2. Benjamin West, his uncle
3. Submarine
4. A "coffer" was a mine. They were considered unfair because there weren't two ships battling it out.
5. John Stevens (his brother-in-law); Stevens took too much time in improving his boat, the *Juliana*.
6. It could go downstream faster and was able to move itself upstream.
7. 32 hours
8. French - submarine; England - mine; United States - steam-powered warship
9. It lowered the costs of goods because it was faster and could move back upstream after depositing goods.
10. Many possible answers: boiler explosions, snags, sandbars, etc.

The United States Declares War on England in 1812 (page 54)
1. Henry Clay
2. Because it was a naval ship, and taking sailors off of it was considered an insult to the nation.
3. He allegedly blotted the sun from the sky; this helped to prove to the Native Americans that magic was on their side.
4. They were members of Congress who wanted war with England. The name was given to them as an insult, but they liked it.
5. Impressment was the taking of sailors off ships and making them serve in the British navy.
6. France and England went to war.
7. American ships were allowed to carry goods between the French West Indies and France.
8. The Native Americans' guns had been made in England; they suspected that the English were secretly arming the Native Americans.
9. Ghent, Belgium
10. William H. Harrison and Andrew Jackson

The Missouri Compromise Is Passed (page 56)
1. They meant that slavery was not good, but they needed slaves to do the work.
2. It is passed by Congress and allows a territory to become a state.
3. Maine
4. The line was 36°30'. It would go across the Louisiana Purchase; the territory south of the line was open to slavery; north of it would be closed to slavery.
5. Jesse Thomas of Illinois
6. Florida; Texas
7. Free African-Americans
8. The area closed to slavery would be larger.
9. It divided between north and south and east and west
10. There was only one political party; people were working together as a nation.

The Election Where Second Place Was Good Enough to Win (page 58)
1. Jefferson and Burr were both Republicans and had the same number of electoral votes.
2. It required that the president and vice president be chosen on separate ballots.
3. Jackson and Clay
4. 354,000
5. Plurality
6. Adams, Crawford, and Calhoun
7. He had suffered a stroke and was still recovering.
8. He would have suspected that they were making a crooked deal behind his back.
9. By a caucus of party leaders in Washington (Notice that left out state party leaders and the public.)
10. Unsuccessful; Jackson supporters were too unhappy to let them get by with anything they wanted to do.

Americans Invest in Internal Improvements (page 60)
1. National Road
2. 30 hours
3. 18 cents
4. Buffalo
5. B & O (Baltimore & Ohio)
6. Boilers on locomotives kept blowing up.
7. It had mechanical trouble that slowed it down.
8. 2.57 horsepower
9. Railroads were cheaper to build and could be used in any weather.
10. 80 mph

A "Man of the People" Is Elected President (page 62)
1. South Carolina; Tennessee
2. Horseshoe Bend and New Orleans
3. Because Rachel was married to Robards and Jackson at the same time
4. Spain; England
5. National Republicans; Democratic Republicans
6. Stealing the 1824 election; buying a billiard table with public money (Actually, he paid for the billiard table out of his own pocket.)
7. Adultery, killing innocent Native Americans, fighting duels
8. 95
9. Many people came from western regions of the country.
10. They thought "King Mob" had taken over the country.

The Five Civilized Tribes Are Moved West (page 64)
1. Northern tribes were smaller and less organized.
2. Sequoyah invented an alphabet using the 85 syllables of the Cherokee language.
3. Cherokees, Chickasaw, Creek, Choctaw, and Seminole
4. Governor George Troup of Georgia
5. William McIntosh; he was killed because he gave up tribal land.
6. The man who was to supply them did not come with the supplies because of the cold weather.
7. Osceola
8. It meant that the Supreme Court had very little power unless the president backed them up.
9. Oklahoma
10. Cherokee

Jackson Declares War on Nullifiers and the Second Bank of the United States (page 66)
1. Nullification said states had the right to block any federal law from being used inside its boundaries.
2. Jackson said he would send an army against it.
3. You can put money in the bank until you need it and can borrow from the bank.
4. The Second Bank kept state banks in check, was a safe place for government money, and made it easier for the federal government to borrow.
5. The Bank was criticized for having too much power and for bribing politicians and newspapers.
6. Nicholas Biddle
7. Henry Clay
8. National Republican
9. He withdrew government funds and did not replace them with revenues. Instead, he put the money in state banks (pet banks).
10. The Bank was rechartered as a Pennsylvania bank in 1836 and shut down in 1841.

Some Slaves Refuse to Give in to Their Masters (page 68)
1. 1807
2. Drivers; overseers
3. Field hands, skilled laborers, and servants
4. They were always in danger of being sold away from their spouse or children.
5. Because when the slave died, he or she would go to heaven.
6. Richmond, Charleston
7. Gabriel
8. Set fires, broke hoes, loafed on the job
9. Nat Turner
10. Douglass fought him and came out on top. Covey never bothered him again.

The North Develops an Industrial Economy (page 70)
1. Inventions require factories to produce, so job opportunities are expanded.
2. Girls were hired from nearby farms.
3. Fathers worried about their daughters and wanted to keep them safe.
4. Eight years old. They received little education because they worked all day.
5. It had the water power necessary for early machines, and farms in New England were poor, so they had a good labor source.
6. They didn't like the low wages, long hours, and constant female companionship.
7. England, Ireland, and Europe
8. Workers knew they could easily be replaced, and that lowered their bargaining power.
9. It was no longer considered necessary because they didn't know the girls' parents, and the girls had no ties to the community.
10. The South thought these conditions were terrible and that the workers were badly treated.

Houston Leads Texans to Independence (page 72)

1. Moses Austin
2. 13,277 acres
3. Cherokee
4. Horseshoe Bend
5. Alamo; Goliad
6. Mexico argued that the boundary was the Nueces River; Texans said it was the Rio Grande.
7. Northerners didn't want a large slaveholding state added to the Union.
8. England, France
9. By joint resolution (They tried to get a treaty, but treaties require a two-thirds vote in the Senate.)
10. John Tyler

Americans Take an Interest in Oregon (page 74)

1. Robert Gray
2. Hudson's Bay Company
3. He read the journal of Lewis and Clark.
4. Whitman and Spalding
5. Independence, Missouri
6. The *Columbia*; he named the river after his ship.
7. Because so many of the ships and sailors came from Boston
8. He received a letter from the governor of California accusing Kelley of being a horse and cattle thief.
9. Organization, having good teams and wagons, and traveling light all helped.
10. 49th parallel

Abolitionists Act, Congress Reacts (page 76)

1. Mann's interest was education. By 1860, every northern state had public schools.
2. Elizabeth Blackwell was the first woman physician in the United States.
3. *Freedom's Journal* was unusual because its editors were African-American. (Samuel Cornish and John Russwurm)
4. Lundy's paper was *The Genius of Universal Emancipation*. Garrison thought Quaker appeals were too slow.
5. It was charged that Nat Turner had read it.
6. Lovejoy was killed by a pro-slave mob in Alton, Illinois.
7. Many abolitionist petitions urged Congress to act against slavery.
8. The Gag Rule tabled these petitions without discussion.
9. The post office destroyed them or refused to deliver them.
10. 1844

Nicholas Trist Makes Peace With Mexico (page 78)

1. Problems included trouble between Santa Fe traders and officials, Texas Revolution, Native American problems, and unpaid debts.
2. Bear Flag Revolt
3. The key phrase was "American blood has been shed on American soil."
4. Abraham Lincoln and John C. Calhoun
5. Taylor at Monterrey, Kearny at Los Angeles, Scott in Mexico City.
6. Trist was there to write a treaty with Mexico. Scott thought he was Polk's spy.
7. Trist had finally found a faction in Mexico willing to make peace.
8. $15,000,000
9. Polk was angry with Trist because he did not obey orders.
10. Polk got even by refusing to pay the money the government owed him. It was not paid until 1871, after his death.

Sutter's Secret Is Told—A Gold Rush Follows (page 80)

1. Fur trappers, whalers, and cattle buyers were the first Americans to go to California.
2. Sutter came to America to avoid paying his debts in Switzerland.
3. Sutter gave them a place to rest and recuperate.
4. The Bidwell party was the first to travel overland to California.
5. The Hastings Cutoff used unverified information.
6. The Donner party got trapped in the mountains and resorted to cannibalism.
7. James Marshall discovered gold.
8. Routes were around South America, across Panama, or overland.
9. The overland route was the most commonly used.
10. Even if they found gold, they had a hard time because of the high prices.

Daniel Webster Delivers the Seventh of March Speech (page 82)

1. Public speaking was one of his weak points.
2. The "Liberty and Union" quote was from when he was speaking against the nullifiers. (Webster-Hayne debate)
3. He supported the Wilmot Proviso because he thought slavery was morally wrong.
4. The South opposed personal liberty laws because it made it difficult to retrieve escaped slaves.
5. The theme was the importance of keeping the nation together.
6. California became a state.
7. New Mexico became a territory and received land from Texas.
8. Texas gave up some land and got $10 million.
9. The slave trade was abolished in the District of Columbia.
10. It made it harder for fugitive slaves to escape.

Uncle Tom's Cabin Is Published (page 84)

1. Lyman and Henry Ward Beecher were famous ministers.
2. Calvin Stowe was a minister and a college professor.
3. She wrote short stories that were published.
4. She visited a plantation in Kentucky. The owners were kind to their slaves.
5. She blamed it on the system; she felt that owners and slaves were trapped by the system.
6. Edward Beecher's wife encouraged her to write against slavery.
7. She wrote the ending first, describing the death of Uncle Tom.
8. Two other slaves: Topsy, Eliza, Quimbo, and Sambo (any two)
9. A "Simon Legree" is cruel and works people to death.
10. *Uncle Tom's Cabin* sold 1.5 million copies in England.

The Nation Focuses on "Bleeding Kansas" (page 86)

1. The reason for the Gadsden Purchase was to build a railroad to California from the South.
2. Douglas wanted the railroad to start from Chicago. He was an Illinois senator.
3. It would make it easier for settlers to get surveyed land and have protection.
4. The Missouri Compromise was overturned; the area north of 36°30' might be open to slavery.
5. A Beecher's Bible was a rifle.
6. Pierce supported it.
7. When elections were called, 5,000 Missourians voted.
8. Brown killed five pro-slave men and boys at Pottawatomie Creek.
9. Republicans blamed the South and the Democrats.
10. Kansas became a state in 1861.

Buchanan Is Elected in 1856 (page 88)

1. Sumner gave a speech; it criticized Andrew Butler.
2. Canes were sent to replace the one broken over Sumner's head.
3. Pierce and Douglas were too involved in the Kansas-Nebraska Act.
4. Buchanan felt that slavery was wrong, but the federal government could not interfere with it in states and territories.
5. Old Whigs joined either the Republicans or the American party. (A few became Democrats in the South but were never happy about it.)
6. SSSB stood for Supreme Order of the Star-Spangled Banner.
7. Members promised to say "I know nothing" whenever anyone asked about the SSSB.
8. Catholics and immigrants
9. Seward and others felt that the Republicans would lose the election.
10. "Free soil, free speech, free men, Frémont" was their slogan.

John Brown Attacks Harpers Ferry (page 90)

1. An abolitionist would oppose the statement about African-American inferiority and lack of rights.
2. Slavery is terrible. If it is good, why doesn't he join the slaves?
3. Helper said they should be concerned about poor whites, not slaves.
4. The Secret Six were Boston abolitionists; they gave Brown $10,000.
5. Brown knew there was a federal arsenal and armory there; it was in the mountains, and he could use it as a base for a slave rebellion.
6. Since it was in a slave state, slaves would go there and join his army.
7. Free African-Americans feared that if it failed (a real possibility), they would be captured and returned to slavery.
8. One of Brown's men shot a free African-American. By allowing the train to leave, it gave the engineer a chance to report what was going on.
9. Colonel Robert E. Lee led the marines.
10. Brown decided that if that was the way it had to be, he would accept it.

South Carolina Secedes (page 92)

1. Southern delegates wanted the party to split; when the Republicans won, they would have a good reason to secede.
2. Southern Democrats chose John C. Breckinridge.
3. Northern Democrats chose Stephen Douglas.
4. William Seward was Lincoln's rival.
5. Republicans promised a railroad to the Pacific.
6. Bell support was in border states.
7. Douglas campaigned asking the South not to secede.
8. Lincoln led Breckinridge by 108 electoral votes.
9. About 1 million more voted against Lincoln than for him.
10. Seven states joined the CSA.

Lincoln Asks for 75,000 Volunteers (page 94)

1. Only Ft. Sumter and Ft. Pickens remained in U.S. hands.
2. The public knew nothing; Lincoln didn't say what policy he would follow.
3. In his inaugural speech, he said that any war would be brought on by the South, not by him.
4. The ship was sent to supply Ft. Sumter, but it was hit by a shell.
5. Beauregard took command of the army there and was to take Ft. Sumter.
6. Beauregard knew the supply ships were on the way, in which case Anderson could stay if they arrived.
7. April 14, 1861, was the date the Confederate flag waved over Ft. Sumter.
8. Four states leaving: Virginia, North Carolina, Tennessee, and Arkansas
9. Four states remaining: Missouri, Maryland, Kentucky, and Delaware
10. Lee opposed slavery and secession. He had always been a U.S. soldier. (You might add that he was a graduate of West Point, a friend of General Scott, and had the chance to lead the U.S. army with a general's rank.)

African-Americans Become Part of the War (page 96)
1. Slaves became free by escaping, being freed by their masters, escaping through the Underground Railroad, or were born free.
2. Most northern African-Americans lived in cities.
3. Lincoln knew that if the South won the war, slaves would remain slaves.
4. The boundary would be the Ohio and Mississippi Rivers.
5. Lincoln wanted to pay owners $400; the idea was turned down.
6. Ben Butler coined the term "contrabands."
7. Lincoln justified taking slaves as a war measure because slaves had been used by the South in the war effort.
8. Two officers of African-American troops: Thomas Higginson and Robert Shaw (Both were from abolitionist backgrounds.)
9. 247 of the 600-man 54th Massachusetts were killed.
10. Patrick Cleburne proposed enlisting African-American soldiers in the Confederate army.

The South Scores Some Wins (page 98)
1. The North had its greatest lead in manufacturing (10–1).
2. Bull Run was the first major land battle.
3. Southern advantages: fighting on own land and good generals
4. Jackson's men showed up, which broke the Union line.
5. Beauregard was in trouble because President Davis wanted him to chase the Union army.
6. Lee sent Jackson toward Washington. That forced Lincoln to take men away from McClellan's army.
7. After Johnston was wounded, Lee replaced him.
8. They were called "foot cavalry" because they moved as fast as men on horseback.
9. McClellan was in trouble because he had not attacked the retreating Confederates.
10. Lee split his army even though they were outnumbered (2–1).

July 4, 1863—A Day of Northern Victories (page 100)
1. Three battles making Grant famous: Ft. Henry, Ft. Donelson, and Shiloh
2. Vicksburg was hard to take because it was on the Mississippi, sat on high bluffs, and overlooked low swamps.
3. By 1863, it was the only spot connecting the eastern and western Confederate States of America.
4. Grant marched into Louisiana, crossed the river south of Vicksburg, captured Jackson, Mississippi, and attacked Vicksburg from the east.
5. People survived by living in caves and eating dogs, cats, and mules.
6. Lee had 75,000 men.
7. Meade had commanded for three days.
8. The most important day was July 3, with Pickett's Charge.
9. Lee escaped because Meade didn't attack until after nearly all of the army had already crossed the Potomac.
10. The South couldn't go on the offensive again because they had lost too many men.

Women Join the War Effort on Both Sides (page 102)
1. Women began to run the farms and work in factories.
2. Clara Barton started the Red Cross.
3. Doctors didn't like them because the women got after them for being lazy or cruel.
4. Greenhow passed information to Beauregard that helped at Bull Run.
5. Bowser worked as a servant at Jefferson Davis's home and fed information to Mrs. Van Lew.
6. Boyd supplied medicine and information to Jackson.
7. Van Lew fed the information she gathered from Union prisoners to Grant.
8. Dix was Superintendent of the U.S. Army Nurses and appealed to private donors for any supplies that were needed.
9. Bickerdyke nursed wounded soldiers and aggravated the doctors.
10. Howe wrote "The Battle Hymn of the Republic."

Booth Kills Lincoln (page 104)
1. Generals unable to stop Sherman: Joe Johnston and John Hood
2. Sherman split the South again.
3. Copperheads tried to stir up anti-war, anti-Lincoln sentiment.
4. Copperheads backed McClellan.
5. Booth liked dramatic plays with swordfighting and a lot of action.
6. Booth's friends included Lewis Powell and George Atzerodt.
7. Booth decided on April 11, the night of Lincoln's speech.
8. Atzerodt was to kill Vice President Johnson, and Powell was to kill Secretary of State Seward.
9. Booth broke his leg in the leap to the stage from Lincoln's box; he fell off-balance.
10. The search took 10 days.

Bragging Contest Answers (pages 105–107)

Convention Room A
1. Christopher Columbus
2. Pocahontas
3. Miles Standish
4. Lord Baltimore
5. John P. Zenger
6. George Washington
7. A Son of Liberty
8 Sam Adams
9. An Apprentice
10. Patrick Henry
11. Ben Franklin
12. Thomas Paine
13. Barry St. Leger
14. Benedict Arnold
15. John Jay
16. John Dickinson
17. Daniel Shays
18. Alexander Hamilton

Convention Room B
1. John Jay
2. Matthew Lyon
3. William Marbury
4. Samuel Slater
5. Toussaint L'Overture
6. Robert Fulton
7. Henry Clay
8. Jesse Thomas
9. John Q. Adams
10. James Madison
11. Andrew Jackson
12. Sequoyah
13. Nicholas Biddle
14. Gabriel
15. John Tyler

Convention Room C
1. John Floyd
2. Horace Mann
3. Winfield Scott
4. Lansford Hastings
5. Daniel Webster
6. Simon Legree
7. David Atchison
8. John Frémont
9. Roger Taney
10. John Bell
11. Robert Anderson
12. Patrick Cleburne
13. Robert E. Lee
14. George Pickett
15. Mary Bickerdyke
16. George Atzerodt

You Decide (pages 108–111)
Answers will vary.

Suggestions for Further Reading

A person wishing to do further reading on any topic has to start somewhere. One suggestion is to read about the subject in a good encyclopedia (either in print or online). At the end of the article, there will often be suggestions for further reading. Go to one of the sources on the list, and you will discover at the back of the book the bibliography that the author has used. Footnotes at the bottom of the page or the end of the chapter of these sources also give clues about where to find more information on a specific subject. Information on specific topics may also be found on the Internet.

Bibliography

The bibliography included here is not complete, but is intended to suggest some good general sources that are often available in school libraries. Students should look for more sources in the digital or physical card catalog at their local public library as well.

GENERAL

American Heritage Illustrated History of the United States, vols. 1–8.
Life History of the United States, vols. 1–5.

COLONIAL HISTORY

Alderman, Clifford. *The Story of the Thirteen Colonies.* Random House, 1966.
American Heritage History of the American Revolution.
Richard K. Morris. *American Revolution.* Lerner Publishers, 1985.
Phelan, Mary Kay. *The Story of the Boston Massacre.* Crowell, 1976.
Tunis, Edwin. *Colonial Living.* Crowell, 1976.

U.S. 1789–1836

Adler, David. *A Picture Book of Thomas Jefferson.* Holiday House, 1990.
American Heritage Illustrated History of the United States: A New Nation.
Fritz, Jean. *The Great Little Madison.* Putnam, 1987.
Kent, Zachary. *John Quincy Adams.* Children's Press, 1987.
Meltzer, Milton. *George Washington and the Birth of Our Nation.* Watts, 1986.
Phelan, Mary Kay. *The Story of the Louisiana Purchase.* Crowell, 1979.

U.S. 1836–1860

American Heritage Illustrated History of the United States: The Frontier.
American Heritage Illustrated History of the United States: The War with Mexico.
Blumberg, R. *The Great American Gold Rush.* Bradbury Press, 1989.
Fritz, Jean. *Make Way for Sam Houston.* Putnam, 1986.
Miller, D.T. *Frederick Douglass and the Fight for Freedom.* Facts on File, 1988.

U.S. 1861–1865

American History Illustrated History of the United States: Civil War.
Freedman, Russell. *Lincoln, a Photobiography.* Clarion, 1987.
Johnson, Neil. *The Battle of Gettysburg.* Four Winds Press, 1989.
Jordan, Robert. *The Civil War.* National Geographic Society, 1982.
Ray, Delia. *A Nation Torn: the Story of How the Civil War Began.* Lodestar, 1990.
Ray, Delia. *Behind the Blue and Gray: the Soldier's Life in the Civil War.* Lodestar, 1991.
Time-Life Series on the Civil War.
Weidhorn, Manfred. *Robert E. Lee.* Atheneum, 1988.